DEAR
BILL
BRYSON

DEAR BILL BRYSON *

Footnotes from a Small Island

BEN AITKEN

iCON

This edition published
in the UK and USA in 2022
by Icon Books Ltd,
Omnibus Business Centre,
39–41 North Road,
London, N7 9DP
email: info@iconbooks.com
www.iconbooks.com

First published in 2015
by Not Bad Books

Sold in the UK, Europe and Asia
by Faber & Faber Ltd,
Bloomsbury House,
74–77 Great Russell Street,
London, WC1B 3DA
or their agents

Distributed in the UK,
Europe and Asia
by Grantham Book Services,
Trent Road, Grantham,
NG31 7XQ

Distributed in the USA
by Publishers Group West,
1700 Fourth Street,
Berkeley, CA 94710

Distributed in Australia and
New Zealand
by Allen & Unwin Pty Ltd,
PO Box 8500,
83 Alexander Street,
Crows Nest, NSW 2065

Distributed in South Africa
by Jonathan Ball,
Office B4,
The District,
41 Sir Lowry Road,
Woodstock, 7925

Distributed in India
by Penguin Books India,
7th Floor, Infinity Tower – C,
DLF Cyber City,
Gurgaon 122002, Haryana

ISBN: 978-178578-825-3

Typeset in Baskerville MT by Marie Doherty

Printed and bound in Great Britain
by Clays Ltd, Elcograf S.p.A.

For my grandparents.

Contents

Preface to this edition

This wasn't meant to be a book. I followed Bryson because I thought it might be a fun and modestly edifying way to spend two months. (How wrong I was.) But as the journey extended, so did my diary entries, and by the time I got to the finish line (i.e. Bill's old house in Norfolk), the prospect of converting the diary entries into something approximating a book became, if not irresistible, then certainly less ridiculous.

When that conversion was complete, I was too bashful to send the first draft to any publishers or agents, so went down the independent route. I raised some money by getting 'I Love Bill' tattooed on my chest, and then unleased my awkward love letter into a world that mostly failed to notice.

I refer to the book as an irreverent homage because in essence that's what it is. It's an homage because it sprung from a place of affection and respect for Bryson and his work. It's irreverent because I didn't think 300 pages of unctuous flattery would do anyone much good. I wanted my journey to feel less like a pilgrimage, and more like an honest conversation with someone who wasn't there.

I mention this (the book being an irreverent homage, rather than a pious and gushing one) to give the more zealous members of Bryson's fan club a chance to back out now, and thereby avoid getting their knickers in a twist. Whereas Bryson is a demi-god of non-fiction, I'm just mucking about in the foothills of mediocrity – and that's on a good day. Nor am I funny. If

I ever seem funny, or write things that seem funny, it is almost always by accident.

But enough pre-emptive apology and excuse. The book is what it is; and if it happens to bring a handful of readers some moments of distraction (from their prevailing worries, from their children, from the prospect of another national lockdown), then as far as I'm concerned its reissue has been justified. If it doesn't, then it hasn't, and I really ought to retrain as a traffic cone.

Needless to say, the Britain observed and recorded in the following pages is not the Britain that might be observed and recorded today. There is no pandemic, no Brexit, no electric scooters, and no old Etonian at the helm. (No, hang on. There *is* an old Etonian at the helm. Just a different one. Which goes to show how things have a curious knack of changing while staying the same.)

Countries – and all they contain and hint at and connote – aren't the best *sitters*. They can't, for the life of them, stay still. But the slipperiness of Britain shouldn't deter any prospective portraitists, because a snapshot will always have value, and a sketch will always tell us something.

What follows is (at base and root and heart) just another set of notes from a small island, albeit a set of notes inspired by, and guided by, one of that island's shiniest jewels – old Billy boy. (Who isn't my biggest fan, by the way, not since I hurdled his back fence the better to deliver a letter.)

Dear Bill Bryson,

Ever since I was a kid, I wanted to be a middle-aged American. I'd go about school wearing white socks and a fanny pack, mouthing off about taxes, telling anyone who would listen about my four-speed lawnmower. I used to tip the dinner ladies 25 per cent, for God's sake.

Why? Well, in a word – you. I first saw you on television when I was about nine and should have been in bed. You were stood in some field, saying how nice it was. But it wasn't what you were saying that impressed me – it was how you were saying it. I liked your voice, Bill. You sounded so understanding, as if you'd agree to any reasonable proposition – 'Excuse me, Bill, but would you mind awfully if I threw an egg at you?' 'Well, I'm mowing the lawn right now, Ben, but how does three o'clock sound?' I asked my mum if we could get you over for a few babysitting shifts. She told me to turn that rubbish off and get to bed.

To be honest, I forgot about you after that. Then I found your book one day, the one inspired by the field, the one you wrote twenty years ago before going back to the States, the one that was a bestseller in charity shops all over Europe.

Long story short, I've decided to retrace your steps. Why? Because I'm bored. Take it from me, there's only so many tacos a guy can serve before he wants to put a pint of salsa down his windpipe.

First stop, Calais. You remember this town, Bill? You've little reason to, I suppose, since you did bugger all here. And the things you did do – well, I can't even be sure you did those either. For example, you say you took a coffee on the Rue de Gaston Papin, but when I asked a local shopkeeper where I might find such a road, she answered with a look that suggested both xenophobia and pity, before telling me that such a road almost certainly doesn't exist, on account of Rue de Gaston Papin meaning Road of the Forgetful Squid, or something equally unlikely.

I've got to say, Bill, I was pretty wound-up. I slammed my copy of *Notes from a Small Island* against the counter and poked the shopkeeper in the eye. I mean, if you were fibbing about Gaston Papin, what else were you fibbing about? Does Milton Keynes even exist?

Disheartened, I asked a passing clergyman how to get back to the ferry terminal. He issued a volley of eloquent, and no doubt instructive, French words, which I pretended to understand perfectly, when, in fact, I understood nothing at all.

I reasoned that the ferry terminal must be near the water, and so headed for the beach, where I found a teenager chain-smoking electronic cigarettes and whispering philosophical maxims to a point in the middle distance. I pointed to the bundle of cranes and freight containers yonder and said, skilfully, and in French, 'Boat?' He shrugged six times and then quoted Jean-Jacques Rousseau, who once said, or so I'm led to believe, 'In autumn there is hope', which I understood to mean that he wasn't at all sure.

I found the ferry without further ado and took up vigil on the viewing deck. The day was bidding adieu, and as the coconut cliffs of Dover began to rise from the Channel's dark soup (overwritten?), I reasoned that things weren't so bad after all – to be on these waves and under this sky and at the dawn of what promised to be an eventful, if unoriginal, journey around a small island. (What's the deal with copyright, by the way?)

Yours,

Ben

1

Calais–Dover

There wasn't really a young man quoting Rousseau; there was no passing clergyman; I did not poke a woman in the eye. I made those things up to get your attention, which is what you're supposed to do at the start of a book. You're also supposed to start with a description of the weather, so I should add that, for the most part, it was overcast in Calais.

I walked from the port into the centre along the Rue Constant Dupont and the Rue Pierre Mullard, street names that seemed elegant and thrilling, despite their essential banality. I passed a pub called Le Liverpool, which looked sad and unpopular. I suppose it was once busy with British day-trippers in shell suits stocking up on Kronenbourg and Côte du Rhône, the sort of people Bryson records seeing a lot of in '94. I wondered about the provenance of this pub. Perhaps, in the late 80s, a canny Frenchman thought he'd cash in by giving the day-trippers a slice of home, understanding that the British tend to go overseas not to escape their culture but to find a warmer or cheaper version of it.

I came to the Place d'Armes, where I made a cursory effort to find a Virgin Mary bedside lamp. (Bryson bought one here, you see, before spending the evening playing with it in his hotel room.) I took a walk up to the old town to see the Rodin sculpture. *The Burghers of Calais* depicts half-a-dozen members of the city's medieval middle class looking fed up, on account of the

King of England having just announced that they were to be executed the following Tuesday. The burghers were eventually pardoned after the King's better half intervened. Rodin has a lesser-known sculpture, elsewhere in Calais, of the men looking relieved.

I took the plat du jour at Au Bureau on the Rue Royal and drank two bottles of Stella Artois and it felt good and warm to be alone and softly drunk. I enjoyed the strange anonymity of being foreign, when one is at once more and less obvious to others, more and less significant. I knew no one in this city; I had no appointments or obligations; I had never cried or laughed or made mistakes here. For all anyone knew, I might have been arrogant or timid or generous or sad. As I reflected on the cleansing effect of travel – that I was once again at the beginning of my character – the beef stew arrived.

On the last ferry to Dover I went up to the viewing deck to enjoy the wind and the dark and to watch Calais recede. A Romanian asked me to take a photograph of him with the cliffs in the background. I told him it was too dark but he said it didn't matter because the cliffs would still be there. He was excited to be returning to England (where he was a student) and told me, after just a few minutes' conversation, that we are just little in this world and that it's pointless to think too much. I told him about Socrates, who said that the unexamined life wasn't worth living. 'His life was worth examining,' replied the Romanian, 'yours isn't.'

The Romanian was probably right, but up on that deck,

passing through that channel, I couldn't help but examine things. In particular, what the hell I was up to travelling again. Bryson had a good reason – he wanted a final glance at Britain before returning to America – but what was my excuse? Was I feeding an addiction? Was I putting off adulthood, with its manifold responsibilities?

Keen for an answer, I thought about Pascal, who held that the principal cause of man's restlessness is that he does not know how to stay quietly in his bedroom. It's easy to read Pascal's maxim as a celebration of doing nothing, but such a reading would be off the mark, I feel. Instead, is Pascal not simply pointing out that people are liable to wander and roam because they routinely fail to notice the pleasures and complexities inherent in those things with which they are most familiar?

One guy read Pascal's celebration of going nowhere perhaps a little too literally. In 1790, Xavier de Maistre spent nine months travelling in his bedroom, rejoicing in the room's hitherto unnoticed charms and associations: a busted mattress spring, for example, brought to mind a particularly robust old flame.

For me, then, Britain is a sort of bedroom. I was born and grew up in this bedroom. I think I know where the cupboard is and how the books are arranged. I know which corners gather most dust and I know which neighbour I can get a cup of sugar from. I know all these things but I know them complacently – lazily – for I stopped paying attention to my bedroom a while ago; it had become so familiar that it no longer seemed to deserve my regard. Was it not time, therefore, to take a look at those busted springs?

But why not take my own journey? Why copy Bryson? Was I not setting myself up for a fall by retracing the journey of a prize-winning supremo when my only writing credit to date was a spell subediting *Family Fortunes*?

Well, pragmatism certainly had something to do with it. First, copying is much easier than devising: not only would I not have to organise an itinerary, I wouldn't even have to decide what to eat each night: if Bill consumed a frankfurter in Dover then I would as well. Second, when the time came to send a few chapters across to the Publishing Industry – to whom I am depressingly unconnected – would my imitation game not appeal to the Marketing Department? I could imagine snippets of the promotional junk: '*Just like Bryson – if you really squint!*' And if I'm honest for a second, I suppose I felt that a younger, less cosy, more British perspective on this small island might not be the worst thing in the world.

When Bryson first visited Dover, back in 1973, he slept in a bus shelter with underpants on his head. He had tried to secure a bed at a guesthouse but was thwarted by the lateness of his arrival and the slightness of his budget.

A short walk from the ferry terminal took me to Marine Parade, where I found Bill's shelter. I took out my copy of *Notes from a Small Island* and read about the sound of Dover's waves and the turning beam of the lighthouse, and about a dog peeing on all upright things while its owner prophesied that the weather would turn out fine, in spite of all signs to the contrary.

Earlier that day, amid London's anxious crowds – who were being herded here and there by unseen shepherds – I had felt lonely and sad. And yet, in a beautiful paradox, here I was, actually alone, in a bus shelter, in Dover, at midnight, on the cusp of two months mimicking a guy from Iowa, unquestionably happy.

I found a room at a nearby guesthouse, where I fell asleep to the sound of lorries rolling out of ferries, each carrying something, each going somewhere: pencils to Swindon, cabbage to the West Riding. I liked my bedroom.

In 1973, streaky bacon was one of the many things in Britain that Bryson had never heard of. Everything was strange and novel to Bill, and thus that much easier to warm to. He liked the way the British used cutlery and called each other 'love' and 'mate'. He liked the way they got excited about tea. And even those things that displeased or confused him had an enchanting effect – all was improved by the gloss of novelty.

At breakfast the next morning, I wondered to what extent naivety is an asset to the traveller; whether my being a lifelong citizen of Britain would make me a worse chronicler of it. But in one sense I certainly was naive. For someone planning to write a book that sought to compare Britain now with Britain in 1994, I knew worryingly little about Britain in 1994. Perhaps this is unsurprising, given that I was eight in 1994, when my interest in current affairs amounted to a sometime concern about whether Keith from around the corner was coming out to play.

That said, I did know that Prince Charles gave up

competitive polo in 1994 and that Great Britain, with typical restraint, won only two bronze medals at the Winter Olympics in Norway, and reasoned that, as points of comparison, these would serve as well as any.

Dover is a seaside town of 50,000 people who mostly pack salad or work for Brittany Ferries. With this useful information in mind, I left the guesthouse and walked along Townwall Street and then up to Dover Castle. At the entrance to the castle's grounds I was asked for £20.

'Can't I just have a look?'

'They all say that.'

'And then what do you say?'

'No.'

I cursed the woman's sentience and yearned aloud for the mindlessness of machinery, which can be easily circumvented or tricked to think that artichokes are bananas. Even at this early stage of my trip I couldn't afford to cough up twenty quid just to verify there was a castle up there. I had saved £1,500 for ten weeks' travel. If I wanted to see such things as Dover Castle I would have to be flexible in my approach. Accordingly, at the rear of the castle's grounds, I hurdled a 4-foot iron fence before making an awkward ascent up a bank matted with fallen leaves, at the top of which was a 30-foot medieval wall, which I hadn't spotted on Google Maps.

Thwarted, I set off instead to see the famous white cliffs. After 30 minutes walking I encountered a pair of ramblers who told me to give up because it was another few miles and they weren't that good anyway. One of the pair was evidently related to Socrates (the aforementioned chatty and thoughtful ancient Greek), because without invitation she commenced a lecture on local fracking, local xenophobia, local salad packing, and local battle re-enactment. At the end of the lecture she took me by the shoulders: 'That'll teach you to talk to strangers.'

It started raining, so I hastened back into town. Because Bill hadn't given me much to do in Dover (an Italian meal, some quiet absorbing, a walk along Marine Parade), I lingered in a gift shop choosing a postcard, hoping the rain would abate. I bought one that depicted the quintessential features of Britain. If the postcard is to be believed, and there's no reason why it shouldn't be, life in Britain is mostly about cricket and seagulls.[1]

And then I took a photograph of Socrates. I hadn't meant to, she just turned up in my viewfinder when I was attempting to frame a seagull playing cricket. She spotted me and enquired if I'd like to join her for another seminar and a cup of hemlock. I kind of stood there dumbstruck for a few seconds, by which time she'd pulled me into a sandwich shop and begun a new monologue about the difficulties faced by young people in the town. When she paused for breath, I turned to a bookseller at a neighbouring table and asked what he'd do with a spare afternoon in Dover. He said he'd probably start alphabetising the Science Fiction section.

Having no such section to alphabetise, I went to London.

---

[1] Oh that it were!

2

London

I was first in London as a seventeen year old. My girlfriend at the time and I stopped there en route to an amusement park near Stoke-on-Trent. About a year later, when said girlfriend was studying medicine at Kings College in London and I was taking a forced gap year, having been rejected from all six of the universities I had applied to, I visited her and we went to see *The Lion King* at the Lyceum and ate at a cheap Italian restaurant on the Thames.

The following autumn I began a degree in literature and theatre at a university twenty miles outside of London. Accordingly, my friends and I would often catch a train into the capital to unburden ourselves of a decent chunk of that term's student loan, and perhaps a little bit of bank credit, should the occasion call for it, which it invariably did.

After graduating I had little idea what to do with my new understanding of dramatic irony, so I copied everyone else and moved into London, taking a box room in Tooting and making ends meet by misguiding GCSE students as to how they might pass their forthcoming exams, and by helping out a guy with cerebral palsy, no doubt with equal ineptitude. (I remember on one occasion distractedly adding a teaspoon of mustard to his hot chocolate. My hourly rate was reduced by 16 per cent the following month, whence it remains.) In the evenings I would review plays, usually small productions out in the suburbs, and it was this toing and froing across London that did most to acquaint me with the city. A Korean adaptation of *Macbeth* in Shepherd's Bush would be followed by a new play about particle physics in Kilburn, and that by a little-known Estonian comedy in Wandsworth, which I guiltily gave four stars, having fallen asleep during a monologue about Soviet beach resorts.

Anyway. That was then. Back to now. And back in particular to a pub near Victoria station called Balls Brothers, where I managed to vex the barman by ordering half a pint of lager and then having the temerity, upon being presented with a full one, to remind him that I had only ordered a half. He sighed in a way that suggested low job satisfaction, and I was reminded how easy it is to upset and be upset in old London town.

I took a table outside and tried to get chatting to my neighbour but the traffic – angry and abundant despite the congestion charge introduced in 2002 – was prohibitive. Big cities, I reflected, with their noise and combustion, make warm casual encounters difficult, a difficulty that over time hardens until it becomes a characteristic. City dwellers, both new and old, instinctively respect this characteristic and so it perpetuates.

Instead of talking to my neighbour, then, I watched people crossing the road urgently and unsafely, each stride desperate, each elbow sharp, each willing to take a hit from a Renault if they must, and raised a glass to lost patience, and lost civility, and to William Wordsworth, who suggested, when he wasn't salivating over a daffodil, that city life pollutes the soul.

I had a reservation at Hazlitt's, where Bryson had stayed twenty years earlier. The hotel has a lot going for it. It's right in the middle of Soho, for a start, close to the house where Mozart and Hendrix lived (on separate occasions); Charles II, when he wasn't taking sabbaticals in France, used to shampoo his horses here; and the hotel's bedrooms are named after William Hazlitt's 'chums or women he shagged or something', to quote Bill. I was told by the receptionist – who I found, after some minutes, under his counter mending a troublesome modem – to unpack my stuff in Mrs Millet, which isn't something one is invited to do every day.

Hazlitt's is also a pretty upmarket hotel, and you might be wondering what a guy like me, who can't afford to take a look at Dover Castle, is doing booking a room at such a place. Well, truth is, for we might as well be straight about these things, I wasn't paying for the room. I wrote to the hotel a few weeks before and explained my intention to copy Bryson's journey and write a book about it, which I would then attempt to get published, suggesting that a renowned publisher had the tentative rights to the book, but declining to add that these rights were so tentative that the publisher wasn't even aware of them. Mea culpa.

After dumping my things, I went and had a cup of tea at a café on Old Compton Street. The sun was blanching all things, robbing the scene of its moment in time – 22nd October 2013 – and lending, in its place, every conceivable decade – it might have been the 30s or the 60s or the 80s sitting on that terrace with that sun making everything pale and burnished and louder. All was silhouette: a rickshaw, a couple holding hands, the tall erect postures of terraced buildings. In such a light the street became a poem, reduced to its essential lines and truths, and I wanted to commit the poem to memory but knew that a syllable or two – nay, whole stanzas – would get lost, and I knew that taking a picture was pointless for no camera could capture what I wanted captured because it was coloured by my mood. Instead, I watched the passing profiles: an Orthodox Jew with red headphones, a beautiful Arab man, a punk, a pensioner, and a woman marching back and forth in summer colours like an uncertain peacock. The diversity pleased me because it promised a wider range of potential experience: who we might kiss, how we might dress, who we might be!

At Leicester Square I looked for a long time at a sous-chef working in the kitchen of a Café Rouge restaurant. Restaurants like to expose their kitchens these days, perhaps to assure punters the chef isn't blowing his nose on slices of cured ham. As the sous-chef salted a pan of mussels, I wondered what allows certain scenes to gain and hold our attention as we pass through a city. There were perhaps a thousand things I might have been drawn to that afternoon – a statue of Shakespeare, a line of buildings on Regent Street, a collision of motorcycles outside the Royal Court Theatre in Sloane Square. What was it about the sous-chef at work in the kitchen of a French chain restaurant that arrested me? Perhaps, having done such work, sympathy drew me toward the kitchen's toil. Perhaps nostalgia had me wanting to return to the fray, to re-enlist, to once more turn meat and slice leek and ladle soup into bowls. Or perhaps it was the sous-chef's peculiar beauty (his nose was somehow rectangular) that attracted me, or the aesthetic puzzle produced by the half-clean windows, the griddle steam, the too-large clock posing silently behind it all.

At Covent Garden I joined a tour group doing a sweep of key sites. Cutting through Trafalgar Square, our guide spoke of Henry VIII and Horatio Nelson and a man called Michael Fagin who, in 1982, managed to break into Buckingham Palace and ask the Queen for a cigarette. At St James's Palace, we paused to watch the preamble to the christening of a boy called George. Our guide asked whether there were any republicans among the group; whether there were people who considered the monarchy a significant waste of dosh, who thought all the pomp and ceremony and primogeniture made a mockery of claims that Britain had made steady intellectual and social progress since Henry VIII was at the helm beheading women for minor infringements. A French girl and I raised uncertain hands.

Outside the House of Commons we learnt that Guy Fawkes was a Catholic and that the wally wrote a letter warning of the forthcoming explosion of Parliament to the only Catholic MP, who duly showed the King. Fawkes was caught in the cellars of Westminster Palace sat on nineteen barrels of gunpowder reading a magazine. He was asked what he was doing sitting on nineteen barrels of gunpowder and he said he was reading a magazine. For being a sarcastic so-and-so he was cut into sections then set ablaze.

On my way back to the hotel I passed through Angel Court, along whose length I counted and photographed thirteen warnings or cautions or dictates, to do with smoking or loitering or littering or playing ball games or parking your bike or letting your dog relieve itself. It's easy to think that the measures taken to suppress crime – and the infringement on individual liberty involved therein – were always more severe in earlier epochs – when Fawkes was set ablaze, for example – but the 30 metres of Angel Court, with its plenitude of threats, suggest we are more policed than ever.

One of the things that Bryson most liked about London were the polite blue notices mounted to certain buildings that explain that Charlie Chaplin once took a bath on this site and so on. He considers such notices – along with cheery red pillar boxes and benches and pedestrian crossings that actually work – 'incidental civilities' that, when experienced together, do a lot to recommend London as a place of calm and steady decency. I do hope that such things don't fall too much out of fashion, that such politeness isn't replaced to too great an extent with the cautionary warnings that characterise Angel Court, for it would be a shame if anxiety got the better of civility, in London or any place.

Bryson wrote that Hazlitt's was enjoyably *unlike* a hotel; that if one phoned down for a bar of soap, for example, one would invariably receive a pot plant. That evening – there being nothing erotic or thrilling on television – I phoned down for some soap.

'Reception.'

'It's Aitken.'

'Who?'

'Look, can you send up a bar of soap?'

'Is there not one—'

'There was, yes. But I've used it already.'

'There should be extra soap under the sink.'

'Yeah, I've used that as well.'

'What have you been— Is everything … *okay*?'

'Sure, things are fine, I just need more soap.'

A few minutes later a nice young woman from Wolverhampton delivered some soap. Now if that isn't progress, I don't know what is.

3

London 2

I felt obliged, the following morning, to have a good wash, given all the fuss I'd made about soap. After checking out, I went in search of the old *Times* building on the Gray's Inn Road, where Bill was a subeditor back in the 80s. Passing through Bloomsbury and cutting across Bedford Square and Southampton Row and Kingsway, I thought a little about Bryson's stated inability 'to understand how Londoners fail to see that they live in the most wonderful city in the world'. One of the reasons Londoners may fail to see their good luck, Bill, is because the existential taxes levied upon them are blinding. The cost of living, the working hours, the commutes, the competition for jobs and resources – such things are depleting, are enervating, so that when one does have disposable time in London it's not uncommon to be too spent to do anything purposeful with it. Dr Johnson reckoned that London had 'all that life can afford', and he may well have been right. But I'm inclined to think that London affords too much of each thing – 250 theatres, 11,000 discos, 93 postmodern exhibitions – so that one is burdened and perplexed by choice, and finally does nothing with their Sunday save for drink tea and watch bad television, just like everyone else in the country. In a sense, then, Londoners – the ones I knock about with anyway – live relatively impoverished lives, in spite of the many wonderful things that, on paper, are afforded them. Hey-ho.

After failing to find the old *Times* building on the Gray's Inn Road, I went to Wapping, taking the tube from Chancery Lane to Tower Hill. Bryson, it would appear, has a soft spot for London's underground network. He enjoys the feeling of being so far down; the smells and the orderliness; the genius of Henry Beck's map, which understood that sequence was more important than scale. Bryson enjoys imagining from below a semi-mythical London above, where Holland Park is full of windmills and Swiss Cottage is a gingerbread dwelling. I sometimes play this game with my friend Anthony (the lad who reduced my wage by 16 per cent). Our version of the game is perhaps a little more down to earth. We don't imagine windmills or gingerbread buildings – cute, beckoning things. Instead, we imagine Baker Street to be full of unemployed butchers, and Tooting Bec a mess of honking cars.

On this morning my tube carriage was full of school kids heading east to Leyton. I spoke with their teacher, who told me about their visit to the Victoria and Albert Museum in Kensington, during which one of the kids had got in trouble for wiping snot on 'Samson Slaying a Philistine' by Giambologna. For some of the kids this was the first time they had been into central London. Their London was elsewhere, he said, where there were no museums or tourists or meetings of Parliament. In their place are fast-food takeaways and pawnbrokers and bookmakers and launderettes and language schools and old-fashioned street markets that do not offer nineteen types of olive. I thought about London's celebrated diversity and asked: How multicultural and meritocratic and liberal can a place purport to be when it is patterned with such firm demarcations, perceived or otherwise?

The Times – and with it Bryson – moved from the Gray's Inn Road to a new site in Wapping in the early 80s. The idea, as far as I understand, was to bring together News International's British interests, to reduce costs, and to implement new printing technology. This last, alongside general cost cutting, would occasion, in 1986, the dismissal of 5,000 staff. Of course things kicked-off, with the dismissed staff and their affiliated trade unions on one side, and everything and everybody representing News International on the other. The conflict, Bryson reports, developed into 'the most bitter and violent industrial dispute yet seen on the streets of London', and saw those that avoided the chop being escorted off the Wapping site after work each day in police convoys. Bryson remembers one unfortunate journalist who had a beer glass smashed in his face by an ex-colleague from Tunbridge Wells who had lost his wine column. The guy nearly died, 'or at the very least failed to enjoy the rest of his evening'.

Bryson also recalls the efforts made by News International to keep up staff morale during the hoo-hah. Each employee received a morale-boosting ration that consisted of a ham sandwich and a warm can of Heineken, a parsimony that almost led, in turn, to further industrial dispute, as members of the Foreign Desk or wherever began drafting placards encouraging management to 'At Least Chill The Flipping Beer', or to 'Put Some Effing Mustard In The Sandwiches'.

Bryson makes his own joke at his former employer's generosity (or lack thereof), imagining a letter sent to his wife in the wake of his death defending the cause of News International. 'Dear Mrs Bryson: In appreciation of your husband's recent tragic death at the hands of a terrifying mob, we would like you to have this sandwich and can of lager. PS – Could you please return his parking pass?'

Bryson returned to Wapping to call on a former colleague, with whom he had arranged to have lunch and compare bald spots. The Wapping site is now redundant and ready for redevelopment as flats, and so if I were to compare bald spots with anyone I would have to go across the street to the shiny new offices, which sit on the fourth floor of Freedom Tower Seven or whatever it's called, part of a plate-glass jungle overbearing a pleasant marina.

Entering the reception area of Freedom Tower Seven, I genuinely had no idea who I would ask to speak to, or indeed what I would say if introduced to someone. ('Er, sorry to bother you Christopher on glossy double spreads, but might I ask how big yours is?') The receptionist asked if I had an appointment. I hadn't. She asked what the nature of my enquiry was. I said it was to do with a trip I was taking that might be of interest. She passed me the receiver and said she was putting me through to the travel editor. I told her quietly that that was a ridiculous thing to do but the receiver was already making a noise.

'Bleach.'

'Sorry?'

'This is Bleach. What is it?'

'I want to pitch a story.'

'Must say this is pretty old school just rocking up.'

'Thank you.'

'So what have you got?'

'Bryson's *Notes From a Small Island*.'

'What about it?'

'Twentieth anniversary of publication.'

'So what?'

'I'm retracing the journey.'

'Has that been done before?'

'No.' I think. 'Same hotels, same sandwiches, same brothels, etc.'

'Don't remember any brothels.'

'You must have the abridged version.'

'Anyway.'

'Anyway. I started in Calais on Monday. Then Dover. Then London. He came to Wapping to compare bald spots with old colleagues. How big is—'

'Look, this is a nice idea, but aren't you setting yourself up for a fall by competing with a legendarily funny writer?'

'Almost certainly.'

'Send me something when you're done. I promise to look at it.'

Four months later, at my journey's end, I sent that something and, as promised, he looked at it. He didn't publish it, but I like to think that he gave it a good long look.

After lunching in the canteen with his pal (who had a smaller one apparently), Bryson takes a walk through the streets of Wapping. Considering the many rows of former wharves and warehouses – now so many apartment buildings – he quivers at the thought of 'these once-proud workplaces filled with braying twits named Selena and Jasper'. In 1960, he tells us, 100,000 people worked on these docks. Yet within twenty years, the tides of commerce and industry now calling for cosmetics and financial derivatives, that figure had declined to exactly none at all. The river, once busy conveying condiments and spices, was now as 'tranquil and undisturbed as a Constable landscape'.

I left that landscape and headed for Waterloo station. Doing so, I entered a fruit-and-veg store and was charged 52p for a banana.

'52p? What comes with it?'

'A receipt.'

'That's the most valuable banana in London.'

'Then aren't you lucky.'

'I daren't eat the thing.'

'Suit yourself.'

'A banana was 7p in 1994.'

'Things change, my friend.'

I came to Waterloo Bridge. As I crossed, it all felt too much. The Shard was there getting longer, and St Paul's was there getting older, and the Shell Building was there getting richer, and the National Theatre was there and so was the London Eye – each bearing over me, each calling my attention, each with their unique stories, dimensions, agendas, materials, residents and employees. About me, it felt, was an impossible encyclo-paedia of endeavour, of going on; an impossible meaningful weight that deserved decoding, that deserved to be borne. But it was all too much. I'd had enough story for one day, enough

London, enough tube and street, enough seen and heard and considered – just enough, thank you. A man played the clarinet, his cloth cap put out for coins. I hadn't the energy to go to my pocket. I closed my eyes and sighed. I walked on.

4

Windsor

The last time I was in Windsor I spent a good portion of the evening in a shopping trolley. When I was studying a few miles away in Egham, a group of us would come into Windsor now and again to make an assessment of the Norman castle, or to feed the swans on the Thames, or to cross the bridge into Eton to ogle the illustrious, or, having exhausted such lowbrow pursuits, to ride down the cobbled slope of Peascod Street on four wheels. At the bottom of Peascod Street, the trolley would usually be steered eastward by a geography undergraduate onto William Street, where there was – and remains – a nightclub called Liquid. We would toss the bouncer a set of keys and tell him to go park the trolley, before heading into the brain-shrinking fuzz of the disco, where we would do what we did best, which was to meditate at great length on the pros and cons of this or that chat up line, without ever dreaming of putting any one of them to use.

The Castle Hotel had kindly agreed to put me up. When Bryson stayed at the hotel he must have been given a room at the far end of the modern extension, for he suggests that its position was 'handy for Reading if I decided to exit through the window'. My room, on the other hand, was centrally located, and far bigger and nicer than anything I deserved. In celebration, I took off my clothes and put on the big television and ran the big bath and opened the big bottle of sparkling water, thinking to add it to the bathtub, because the more bubbles the better, right?

That done, I experimented with the basket of lotions and gadgets which perched mysteriously and invitingly on the cistern, rubbing this here and exfoliating that there, while retaining the good sense, amid this orgasm of self-improvement, to pop the complimentary shower cap in my backpack, in case, as was forecast, it rained the next day. When, some hours later, I stepped out into Windsor's regal air to see what the town did with itself on a Thursday evening, strike me down if I didn't look like Brigitte Bardot.

I met an uptight Spaniard in the Duchess of Cambridge, had a bowl of soup somewhere else, and then wandered over to the old train station, now a pleasant-enough collection of luxury soap shops and chain restaurants, where I had three pints of lager in a Slug and Lettuce. Returning up Peascod Street toward the hotel, I knew full well that I couldn't possibly carry on my evening at Liquid nightclub, not on my own, not on a Thursday, and not when I'd already had enough to drink and needed to be up in the morning to take advantage of the cooked breakfast and walk five miles to Virginia Water with a shower cap on. No, that would be reckless and inappropriate and suggestive of a weak personality. Besides, the place would be full of students and pleasure-starved locals trying to forget that they work in recruitment or the PR department at Legoland. And I wouldn't know any of the songs, or any of the fashionable dance moves, or what drinks were on promotion. My having lived for 27 years was probably in contravention of the dress code. No, I couldn't go to Liquid.

I tossed the bouncer my keys and asked him to go park my trolley. Climbing the stairs to the main disco, I was delighted with my decision. Within minutes of entering said main disco, I wasn't. There were 50 or so people affecting to dance, each in skinny jeans or skinny skirt, each made otherworldly by cream and wax and spray, each moving like a difficult worm, the boys on one side of the room, like the Montagues, deep in shallow shouted conversation as to how best to approach this or that difficult worm in the skinny skirt. What is it that stops them asking, that stops us all asking, I like you do you like me too?

I go to the V.I.P. area and explain to the guy whose job it is to decide who is and isn't very important that I am looking for somewhere quieter where I can perhaps read a chapter of my book. Try Slough, he says. With a bit of encouragement he admits me to a garish lounge where the drinks are 40p more expensive. But there is no music, and so I read. I read about Bryson holding up Princess Diana in Windsor Great Park and as I begin to slide into the warm cuddle of his prose, I am approached by a teenage version of Hugh Grant.

'I like your niche,' says Hugh.

'Huh?'

'You're not actually reading that book.'

'No?'

'It's an angle. You've read *The Game* by Neil Strauss, right?'

'No.'

'You're lying. What you're doing is explained in chapter seven. You're at once making yourself available and unavailable while appearing clever. Where'd you get the book, anyway?

Was it just lying around?' He inspects it. 'Mistake. If you're reading about travel, makes you seem non-committal. Drink?'

It's kind of unnerving eating breakfast alone in a hotel. For one, there are so many things on the table, most of which are tricky to identify, especially when you've nobody to consult with. I'm pretty sure some of the gear from the bathroom – the little pots of cream and lotion – are put out with the breakfast things, to give the impression of abundance and luxury. Another thing is that the other guests are always so fascinated by you. They're so bored of each other that all of a sudden you're the most intriguing thing in the world. Is his girlfriend still in bed? they whisper. He can't be here on *business*? He's not actually reading that book – it's a niche. Look, Ted, he's dunking his sausage in moisturiser.

Before walking to Windsor Great Park, I had to investigate the shops. I went across to the jumble of cobbled streets opposite the hotel. Market Cross House is still there, leaning severely, as if trying to get out of the way of something, and Woods of Windsor is still selling a lot of lavender cushions and oven gloves. The latter used to purvey something very different, of course. In the 1800s this part of town was stupidly congested with brothels. Apparently one couldn't walk the dog without being encouraged to have three goes for the price of two. I kept an eye open now for the legacy of such an industry, and wondered whether the stiff competition faced by the ladies drove up standards – better lingerie, learning aids, etc. – as is suggested to be the case with schools and hospitals and energy suppliers.

I went into a shop called Glorious Britain, where I found shortbread, Paddington Bear, teabags and a thousand varieties of mobile phone cover, each variation contributing to the illusion that we're all wonderfully and colourfully different when, in truth, the crux of our behaviour is depressingly uniform. Throughout the shop, whether on a coaster or apron or pair of underpants, was the instruction to Keep Calm and Carry On. This ubiquitous appeal to remain relaxed at all costs might well be suitable and effective when applied to a particularly tense game of bowls or snooker, but for almost any other scenario – war, oncoming traffic – the call to Keep Calm and Carry On seems wildly inappropriate. When you think about it, so much of the behaviour considered to be typically British – queuing, emotional reserve, tolerance – might well owe its genesis to an errant batch of tea towels bearing the Keep Calm slogan that were intended for some placid and inconsequential place like Australia but somehow wound up in the Romford branch of Debenhams.

It's easy to attract suspicion when you walk along a high street in a curious fashion. By this I don't mean that one's way of walking is curious, but that one displays curiosity while walking. It is a gentle type of suspicion one attracts – the odd quizzical glance or whispered comment – but it is sufficient nonetheless to discourage us from taking a proper look at the paving or the statues or the stonemasonry above the shop fronts. A child wouldn't behave in this way. If a child is curious about something – a discarded lottery ticket, a piece of Norman architecture – they make sure to have a damn good look. And why the hell not?

It wasn't fear of attracting suspicion that stopped me having a look at Eton College. I know I said earlier that I would occasionally go across the river to Eton to ogle the illustrious, but I was lying. I have never visited Eton and never will, on account of the school's refusal of my application – submitted as a social climbing ten year old – to study there. Had I been accepted, I fancy, I would now be dating Pippa Middleton and writing a column about horses in the *Telegraph*. As it is, I work in a tin mine and can't count beyond seven. No, for all the things that have been denied me – numeracy, Pippa Middleton – I would not be visiting Eton. Besides, I didn't have a clue how to get there from St Leonards Road.

Time was getting on and I still had many miles of walking ahead of me before dusk. Collecting my backpack from the hotel, I was encouraged to have a quick word with the manager, which didn't please me much, on account of the fact that I was carrying a bag full of his merchandise and had told a white lie about my prospects of being published. But, alas, Sam was already beckoning me from an armchair in the corner of the foyer. For a few tense minutes, Sam flicked through *Notes from a Small Island*, as if trying to decide whether he'd made a terrible error of judgment.

'Mr Bryson calls my hotel hig-gle-dy pig-gle-dy. Is this a good assessment?'

'More or less.'

'I see.' He closes the book and balances it on his left palm, as if weighing up its use value. 'And to what extent will my hotel benefit from your publication?'

'Well it was nice meeting you, sir, mustn't chat all afternoon—'

'I would like a figure, Mr Aitken. A hotel manager doesn't thrive because he is a lover of the arts.'

'A figure?'

'I'd like to know how many extra visitors I'm likely to receive.'

'That's a very philosophical question, Samir.'

'No it isn't.'

'At this stage I can only promise two things: to keep you informed about the project, and to make excellent use of the shower cap and slippers.'

Windsor Great Park, according to Bryson, enjoys a 'merciful obscurity', considering how lovely it is and how close to central London. On this particular afternoon I had all three miles of the Long Walk to myself. At the end of the walk you reach Snow Hill, where there is a statue of George III on a horse. Bill describes the view from under the horse's nuts as 'one of the most comely views in England', which probably tells us more about Bill than it does the view.

A short way beyond Snow Hill is Smith's Lawn, a large flat expanse of grass that's mostly used for polo. At one end of the lawn is the Guards Polo Club, an illustrious set-up whose president takes time off occasionally to be the Queen's other half, and wherein I hoped to use the toilet.

Entering the club, I quickly realised that this wasn't the sort of joint where you just popped in to use the loo. I was quickly approached by someone setting up for a wedding. Not bold enough to say what I really wanted (it suddenly felt like needing the toilet was something only peasants did) I wondered whether there was someone with whom I could discuss membership, hoping, of course, that there wasn't. There was, and I was sent through to her office, where she had my number straight away.

'What would you like, to use the toilet?'

'Don't be ridiculous. No, I'd like to become a member.'

'Do you know any present members?'

'Not personally, no.'

'Do you play polo?'

'Not personally, no.'

'Do you own a horse?'

'Look, what you have to understand, Philippa—'

'Let's not mess about, are you royal?'

'Is the Pope a Catholic?'

'So you're royal?'

'No.'

She sighed. 'Could anyone provide a *very* strong character reference?'

I spent another hour or so wandering in the park, keeping an eye open for Fort Belvedere (the former royal residence where Edward VIII abdicated in 1936, an act that paved the way for his younger brother George to star in a 2011 Oscar-winning film), and reflecting on my previous experiences here. Two stood out. Once, during my final year at university, I jogged around the perimeter of the park with a German pianist called Boris, whose cycling shorts did little to disguise what key he was in. And on another occasion, I came to the park at dawn to lark about with a drama student from Birmingham, an experience which encouraged them, just days later, to start going steady with one of my friends.

I let these memories linger as I carried calmly on through the colours of autumn toward the Christchurch Road, which I knew would lead me to Virginia Water, where Bryson fell in love.

5

Virginia Water

Bill first went to Virginia Water to visit two American nurses, which is about as good a reason as any. With the intention of flying back to America the next day to carry on with his studies, Bryson settled down with the nurses to a few pints at the Rose and Crown, perhaps with a view to getting drunk enough that various medical procedures would have to be practiced on him, but not so drunk that he couldn't enjoy them.

In any case, it was after the fourth or fifth pint at the Rose and Crown that Bryson began filling out an application to work at the same psychiatric hospital as the nurses, his handwriting growing so peculiar and addled that the application was almost mistaken by a clerical intern as a plea for admission.

Within hours, Bill was checking in to Male Hostel B; writing to his parents saying not to 'wait supper'; allowing an entire ward of patients to escape while he searched for antacids; and having cricket demystified by a man wanted by the Russians.

About a week into the job Bryson was dispatched to the Florence Nightingale ward to fetch a sedative, where he first encountered his future wife, restraining a kleptomaniac. After an initial, blushing conversation that continued for some minutes – in which time the patient requiring the sedative had climbed out of a window and boarded a bus to Sunningdale – Bryson came to see just how skilfully and patiently the pretty young nurse before him was able to deal with her charges

– 'guiding them to a chair, brightening their day with chatter, wiping dribble from their chins' – and was left with no option but to conclude that, you know what, 'this is *just* the sort of person I need'. Sixteen months later they were married.

The vows were taken at a nearby church, which I passed now as I continued down the main road that runs into the village from Windsor Great Park. Putting aside my worries about having to find (if my emulation of Bryson was to be faithful) a wife within the next few hours, I focused instead on the heavily fortified mansions around me, each one so thoroughly secured that you'd be forgiven for thinking that a siege on a par with Troy had been forecast for the following weekend.

This part of Virginia Water is known as the Wentworth Estate, and comprises a few hundred mega-houses and several golf courses. I knew the area quite well. Not because I had ever been invited into any of the properties, or knew anyone that had, but because I had once been paid £4 an hour to wear a high-visibility tunic and control traffic during a professional golf tournament being held on the estate. At the end of the fourth day, as all eyes were on the tournament's leaders battling it out on the eighteenth green, a history undergraduate and I, making our way off the estate in a Fiat Punto, took a few minutes to play approach shots to the par-three second, my playing partner taking the biggest divot (out of the most immaculate fairway) one could ever care to see. Having attended a decent school in the south of England, he did, however, make a point of replacing it.

On this occasion I stayed away from the golf course and went directly to the village centre, where there are two parades of shops, put up in the 20s and 30s, selling the kind of stuff that only half a percentile of the British population either needs or can afford, like organic salmon cat food. The estate agents on the parade provides an idea of the money in the area. I went inside and spoke with a young man who told me, with a grin that suggested commission, that Virginia Water was the first settlement outside of London where the average house price climbed above a million.

I popped into the Corals betting shop to ask where the Holloway Sanatorium was. I was confident that the guy behind the counter would be able to point me in the right direction, because they usually get Royal Holloway students working at Corals, and the sanatorium was funded by the same Thomas Holloway that lends his name to the university. In fact, a good friend of mine used to work at Corals before he got fired for giving odds of ten to one for all scenarios, including his own dismissal and subsequent fall into alcoholism. Alas, the guy behind the counter neither remembered my friend nor had a clue about the sanatorium, so I needn't have bothered going in really, though he did give me odds of ten to one that someone in the organic salmon shop would know.

And they did, and so I made my way towards the sanatorium, but got only as far as the front gate of the Virginia Park luxury housing estate, the very one that Bill was so impressed by when he came across it twenty years ago. Back then the estate was in its infancy – a few show homes and the like, built around the old sanatorium. Now the houses are all prosperously occupied, with convertible cars in the driveways and not a kid in sight, for it is one of the few inarguable delights of being rich that you can bring kids into your life and then have nothing to do with them until they start making money or running the country.

So I didn't get to see Holloway's famous sanatorium, which was a shame, because by all accounts the building is a real gem, considered by those who know about these things to represent the summit of High Victorian architecture. Befitting its clientele, the sanatorium has a colourful history. Back in the 1860s Lord Shaftesbury started mouthing off about the need for a hospital for the 'insane of the middle class', and hoped to raise five grand or so to get the project off the ground. Thomas Holloway, who obviously had some middle-class relatives to offload, promised 50 times that amount. A call was put out to architects to submit designs. Ten were received. The winner, one W.H. Crossland, received a prize of 200 quid, with the also-rans getting 50 quid for their trouble, except, that is, a Mr Hine from Nottingham, who only got 25, presumably because he ignored the brief completely and designed a bridge or something. There's a lot of chat these days about the sanatorium paying homage to gorgeous buildings in Belgium and Paris, but the truth is that Crossland simply recycled his designs for Rochdale town hall. I am no psychiatrist, but is being reminded of Rochdale going to do much for one's mental health?

I sought out the Rose and Crown, where I hoped to run into a few nurses and maybe complete a drunken application for a life-changing work placement. Heading there, along the Stroude Road, I passed a retirement home called Sunrise, which struck me as a rather inappropriate name for a place where you go to expire. It was now very dark and the directions I had been given were proving equally inappropriate, the corner around which the pub was meant to be turning out to have much more around it than just the pub, another four kilometres, for example.

I ate a steak and kidney pudding and drank a pint of ale as my phone charged. I was keen to make a few calls, as I still hadn't sorted out a place to stay for the night. Bill stayed a couple of miles down the road in Egham, with his mother-in-law. Apparently she sorted him out with a steaming pile of food and some coffee and chatted to him soothingly about work and the kids and what it's like to be a widow. I had a mind to start asking around for this Mrs Billen, and get some of the same treatment. There's rather a touching moment when Bill writes about the times he would go over to Mrs Billen's in Egham and sit with his young fiancée and her family in a warm lounge, just chewing the fat or watching TV. Bill suggests that this kind of experience was new to him, confessing, rather sadly I feel, to having not seen his own family 'in what might be called a social setting since about 1958, apart from a few awkward hours at Christmases'. It's a rare moment when the reader is afforded a glimpse behind Bryson's literary persona – clumsy, optimistic, happy-go-lucky – into something deeper and more plaintive. I don't know, it just touched me somehow, that small comment about his family, about how nice it was to spend time in a warm lounge in Egham watching *The Generation Game*.

Done with my pudding, I got on the blower. A girl from Madrid, who was at university with me, and who now taught in the area, agreed to host me. I took a train to Egham, then took a familiar walk by familiar streets, passing the house I shared in my second year – where I learnt how to skin a rabbit and use a washing line – and then a restaurant called Favourite Chicken, where I had many fine meals and where the guy who took the big divot out of the immaculate fairway worked for a few months before taking a pay cut to move to the BBC. I passed – climbing Egham Hill now, up to the university – the drama department where, having been turned down by eleven universities for being honest about my credentials, I gave such a convincing performance of someone who knew what they were talking about that the interviewing professor was obliged to admit me, a decision that would shape the next ten years of my life.

Royal Holloway's main university building is Founder's Hall, which was designed by the same guy who put up the sanatorium, and is perhaps the finest place for a student to be housed in the country. The architect is remembered by a student bar called Crosslands, where I had arranged to meet Natalie, the girl from Madrid. The bar, I noticed, had experienced some small changes since the spring of 2008, when I would come here most evenings to try and make sense of *Troilus and Cressida*. There was now wallpaper and carpet and furniture that looked as if it might endure more than a term, while the most straightforward sandwich available was now Chorizo and Burnt Tomato Salsa, whereas, back in my day, you were lucky to get bread with your sandwich. In short, things had gotten a lot worse.

Natalie arrived and we drank pints of lager outside at a picnic bench. Had I wished to, I could have whistled up to my old bedroom to get the attention of the present occupant, who might have been from Wrexham or Southend or Coventry or Korea, studying Film or Physics or French or Computer Engineering. I could have whistled up and called them down for a pint, so I could tell them what a brief blessing it was to live in this glorious building, to be nineteen and away from home, meeting new people and learning new things, like how it really isn't necessary to wash colours and whites separately, or how to prepare a meal with only a kettle and a pint glass, or how to cope with unrequited love and iambic pentameter on the same afternoon.

We went to a pub called The Happy Man just across the A30 in Englefield Green, where we met up with Natalie's fiancé, Paul. I can't remember what the three of us spoke about in the beer garden of The Happy Man, but I do remember that the conversation was pleasant, and that walking home with Natalie and Paul and having a nightcap back at their place and learning that Natalie's father translated Shakespeare's sonnets was all very pleasant too. I'll thank the two of them now, if I might, for their unplanned kindness and for presenting an image of committed domestic happiness to work against my instinctive cynicism about long-term relationships, and for reminding me why we should call old friends now and again to tell them we're coming over whether they like it or not, and for allowing me the spare sausage in the morning, on the grounds that it would serve me well on my way to Bournemouth.

6

Bournemouth–Christchurch

And so to Bournemouth. But not before a six-hour delay, on account of stormy weather the night before, which had blown the hat of a signalman in Ipswich onto the track, where it remained, despite the mobilisation of a thinktank and the patience of the rest of the country.

I had a scotch egg as I waited on the concourse at London Waterloo. The scotch egg had caramelised onion and stilton between its nucleus and membrane. Britain has come a long way, I thought, as I broke the membrane and watched a block of commuters stare at the departure boards for fresh information about the blown off hat. Occasionally one would turn to another to give a knowing look, or to raise their eyebrows, or to ask why they didn't just use a fishing rod, but mostly they stood and watched and waited.

Bryson arrived at Bournemouth train station in driving rain and headed directly for the East Cliff, a neighbourhood of medium-sized hotels of which he selected one because the sign was pink. After a typically bothersome check in, Bill's first act is to run a long bath. Having tipped the contents of every sachet and bottle he could find into the tub, Bill sinks beneath a quantity of foam 'seldom seen outside Joan Collins movies', where he remains, if pages can be taken as an indicator of time, for about seventeen hours.

For my part, I stayed on a stranger's couch in Bournemouth,

which is easier to do than it sounds. Couch-surfing is now an established method of securing accommodation, having launched as an online hospitality exchange community ten years ago. You set up a profile, make up something about wanting to live each day as if it were the last, list a whole bunch of books you haven't read, and then start shooting out requests to stay on couches across the world. Needless to say, some couches turn out to be better than others. In Malmö, for example, a friend and I were put to bed in a storage cupboard, full of old carpet and ironing boards and camping gear, to say nothing of the dust, which was sufficient to send my friend's eczema into overdrive. In Jakarta, though, where we stayed with a woman who lobbies the government, the conditions were palatial. We stayed in a large, detached house, protected from the surrounding slums by high walls, and had meals prepared for us by a team of domestic staff who probably earned a dollar a decade or something. For the most part I prefer to whinge about such things as extreme wealth, but on this occasion, having spent the previous fortnight constipated crossing Indonesia on rickety trains, I was willing to give gross inequality a fair trial.

I was collected from Bournemouth station by a university student called Ria. We took the bus to Winton, where Ria lives with three friends. It being late, I wanted nothing but to stay in and drink wine and perhaps take a three-page bath. I certainly didn't have the urge to go out again, but, having missed a day to bad weather, I reasoned that it was somehow my duty to head into town and have a wander around.

My bus dropped me close to the (Lower) Pleasure Gardens. Despite being yards from the sea and in a sensitive mood, I couldn't taste salt in the air, or hear seagulls bickering over a chip, or detect anything else that might usefully have provided a sense of place. I walked without purpose up deserted shopping streets until I came to a corner building that looked vaguely art deco, which I assumed, rightly, to be the home of the *Bournemouth Evening Echo*, and by extension where Bryson spent two long years as subeditor of the Women's Institute's reports.

As is the fashion, the newspaper has outsourced its printing and trimmed its payroll, and now occupies just the top floor of the building. On the ground floor is a bar and restaurant called The Printroom, which pays tasteful homage to the industry that made way for it by displaying front pages of bygone editions and the experimental lithographs of local students. It was beneath one such front page that I whiled away the remains of the day.

Relative to other places in Britain, Bournemouth hasn't been around long. The first properties were put up in the early 19th century by a retired army officer who couldn't bear doing crosswords all day and so built a seaside resort instead. The retired officer skilfully pandered to the superstitions of the time by promoting the health benefits of sea bathing and by planting a bunch of pine trees, the scent of which was thought to be medicinal. The town's first hotels went up soon after, but no one came to occupy them. At the same time in London, struggling travel writer Augustus Granville was of the opinion that he could do with a short holiday, and so wrote to the officer suggesting an all-expenses-paid weekend, which he would then write a glowing report about in fashionable prose. The stunt paid off for both parties. Granville's report was published as a part of a larger book called *The Spas of England*, and Bournemouth's popularity grew steadily thereafter. The officer, incidentally, died suddenly and painfully one summer evening, when a pine tree fell on him.

I was told all this on the bus into town the following morning by an older lady who has lived in Bournemouth all her life, so if there are any factual errors in the above account, the reader has my permission to seek out the aforementioned and take it up with her. I alighted at the bottom of Holdenhurst Road, where I picked up the main shopping street – Christchurch Road – which seemed to be ticking over nicely. These days, if all of a high street's retail units are occupied, no matter the nature of the business or the amount of custom they're attracting, that high street can consider itself in robust health. 'To Let' signs are depressingly ubiquitous on British high streets nowadays, each one a sad admission that things aren't how they once were, when busy housewives bought loaves here and joints there and lemons someplace else, and young couples emerged from the novelty of an Italian restaurant to go see the latest picture, an adaptation of John Braine's *Room at the Top*, perhaps, or *Roman Holiday* starring Gregory Peck and Audrey Hepburn.

Back in '94, Bryson noted a lack of independent coffee bars in Bournemouth, which used to be ten-a-penny when he was working at the *Echo*. Starbucks and the like have had a profound impact on the coffee market, of course, squeezing out smaller establishments all over the country since they entered stage right in the 90s with their bright façades and superlative variations of white with one sugar. As with smartphone covers, it is but the illusion of choice being offered; to enter Starbucks is to tacitly admit to being just like everyone else, no matter the syrup flavour.

That said, there has been an appreciable resurgence of independent coffee shops over the last decade, each with a focus on quality and character, rather than quantity and profit. South Coast Roast on Richmond Hill, where they extract avant-garde blends and play Hank Williams records, is a fine example. Quite the hipster, I had a flat white there and breezed through an e-copy of Hannah Arendt's *The Human Condition (and Other Short Stories)*.

Following Bill's itinerary, I rode a bus to the big Sainsbury's in Someford, whence I followed a sequence of residential streets down to Highcliffe Castle, former home of Gordon Selfridge, the erstwhile retail magnate, whose life, according to Bill, offers a 'salutary moral lesson' to us all – which, in short, is that if your wife dies and you take up such hobbies as gambling and twins, and blow all your capital on both, you'll end up living in Putney.

In '94, the castle was no more than a 'Gothic shell', trapped in a 'parlous and neglected state', without a gift shop or cream tea in sight. Since then, the castle has been restored and opened to visitors, keen, no doubt, to see where Gordon entertained his identical flatmates. The beach below the castle, which I reached by way of a flight of wooden steps, was busy with excited dogs and children crunching across the stones, their owners trailing behind, hands busy with chips or tennis balls, their conversation to do with veganism or the Liberal Democrats or the price of boarding schools.

Further along was the sweep of beach huts spotted by Bryson, 'of identical design but painted in varying bright hues', a description which suggests, as with coffee and phone covers, that we're all doing the same stuff just in different colours.

Outside one hut sat a couple; perhaps the same couple that, twenty years before, prompted Bill to suggest that because they require so little to be so – a biscuit, for example, or a small tax rebate – the British are an unusually happy bunch. He compares the modest needs of the British with American attitudes to pleasure, for whom gratification, 'instant and lavish, is a birthright'. I haven't been much in the States, and certainly not enough to deduce what makes them tick, but I have just started reading Jack Kerouac's *On the Road*, wherein there has already been enough inventive sex and apple pie with ice cream to bear out Bryson's contention that Americans like things big and quick.

I passed the couple outside the hut without stopping, obeying a silly fear that my interest in them might be unwelcome. Then I turned back, suddenly annoyed with my timidity, suddenly confident that people are generally happy to be spoken to – particularly if they've been sitting outside a beach hut for six days.

'Do you mind my asking—'

'No we don't mind!' they said in unison. 'Do we, love? Not at all! Been sat out here since 2001. What's your concern?'

'I'm wondering how you get hold of one of these huts.'

'Waiting list. Big one. Why do you ask?'

'I wouldn't mind putting my mother in one for a year or so.'

They fell silent; looked to the ocean; looked to me. 'Can she spare the time?'

I continued west along the shore, pleased that Bryson's observation about the British being a happy bunch seemed true enough. But it can be difficult to tell that the British are happy, can't it? Sure, you'll overhear jokes and banter and the delighted reception of hot drinks and basic confections – 'Ooh, lovely!' – but to a large extent British happiness is hidden. If it's a British characteristic to be friendly and curious, it's as much a British characteristic to inhibit such qualities, believing it polite to do so. As a result, British friendliness too often fails to escape the clutch of British manners. Thankfully, as we get older we start to see the madness in all this and, with one foot in the grave, adopt an attitude of, 'hell, if I've a question to ask or something to say then I jolly well shall', and start once more to act with the candour and curiosity of children. It is during our middle decades, when we are supposedly most vital, that we are arguably at our most socially inept.

Close to Christchurch Harbour, the sun getting low now, seagulls pushing around in flaps, a boy emptied a bucket of just-caught crabs onto the floor with a view to jumping on them.

'Felix! You will not jump on those crabs!'

'But you said I could!'

'Well now I've changed my mind.'

The boy looked down at his crabs – gasping and desperate – and then up at his mother. 'That's *deception*.'

A short walk inland brought me to Mudeford. Just past the Working Men's Club there is an opening on the left which gives a view of ponies grazing on a soft peninsula, a score of rowing boats bobbing neatly nearby. I sought direction to Christchurch from a couple sat on a bench, who told me that I needed to take a left after the Scouts' Hut, to cross Stanpit Marsh, to pass round the back of some council houses and then skirt the golf course until I came to the confluence of the Avon and Stour rivers, from where I'd see the town a little way off. It was this confluence, they told me, along with the narrow mouth of the harbour, which made Christchurch, back in the day, a decent site on which to set up camp, and also a haven for smugglers returning from France with great wheels of Brie.

I emerged in the car park of Christchurch Council, where I took some leaflets about a wildlife sanctuary and forthcoming changes to the recycling timetable. I spent some moments amid the ruins of a Norman house, and then the ruins of an adjacent bowling green, the latter an increasingly common sight on these shores, as the old enthusiasts die off and the younger generations show no interest in pastimes that can't be uploaded.

I went up to the keep of the ruined 12th-century castle, destroyed by Cromwell during the Civil War so his enemies wouldn't, should they manage to capture the town, have a decent place to crash. From the keep I could peer into the rear windows of Georgian buildings, now a pet shop, a chocolate shop, a Chinese restaurant.

At the harbour, I ate an apple and read one of the leaflets I had taken from the council about a £5-festival taking place that weekend; an initiative designed to get each Christchurch resident to spend £5 on the high street. Apparently, the council were saying, one haircut or quiche or hanging basket a week from each resident would amount to £8 million in annual revenue, sufficient to keep the town centre nicely ticking over, in spite of out-of-town competition. If our ailing high streets are to be revived, such creative interventions are vital.

As it happens, I spent close to £5 on a bus ride to Boscombe, where I bought a can of Becks from an off-licence and proceeded south on Sea Road until I reached Boscombe Pier, where I turned right and continued through a narrow, seaside park toward East Cliff Drive. The park was mostly unlit, and the resultant dark was of the deepest sort. I am not a coward but I am not the bravest either, and ordinarily such darkness in such a place at such a time would have made me uneasy, but for the time being I was fearless, as I couldn't imagine anyone doing me harm, not tonight, not on a day when children had threatened to jump on crabs and people in love had sat before the sea and shared biscuits.

Up on the cliff now, I leant on a white fence and searched in the darkness for Poole Bay, and the crumbly cliffs and the wide golden beaches and the piers and the ships, but could see nothing but the night. It was on this very spot that Bryson began to wonder whether he was making a mistake by returning to the States, by turning his back on friendly shopkeepers and pub fires and views like this one over Poole Bay. But then he remembered hosepipe bans after months of rain, and VAT at 17.5 per cent, and the fact that most Americans believe they've been abducted by aliens, and thereby reached the conclusion that, you know what, it's time I went home, if only to slap some sense into my people.

Behind me, the Suncliff Hotel was lit and seemed warm, and through its large front windows I could see a man entertaining people with an electric guitar. I went inside and took a seat at the bar, where I ordered a Carling and watched the old and young dance and clap, and all those in between, self-conscious or bored, sit on the edge of things, planning their next cigarette. I watched it all – the joy and the dancing and the boredom – and it nearly had me in tears. Let the adults sulk, I thought; it is the children – of all ages – who know what life is for.

7

Salisbury–Stonehenge

My first task in Salisbury was to find the Milford Hall Hotel. I crossed the market square, which was busy having a good portion of it turned into a car park. There was certainly no market going on, as there was when Bill was here, so I was spared the downtrodden lettuce leaves and ironing board covers and tea towels and doormats and upended crates – all those unfortunate tokens of the British market that Bill writes of. But perhaps things have changed. Perhaps it's now pak choi leaves and artichoke hearts and sheets of Serrano ham that are downtrodden in Salisbury. I couldn't say, for there was no market.

I checked in quickly, ate the biscuits, stowed my bag, and then went looking for the office of the local newspaper, where, at 16.30, and twenty years earlier, Bill had met with his old colleague Peter Blacklock. I thought I'd keep the appointment, on the off-chance that Peter still worked at the paper and wanted to have me over to his house to drink brandy and share stories about the good old days. The office was shut.

I walked up Milford and down Chipper and along Minster Streets, stopping to mark a pair of forgotten red phone boxes which, depending on your frame of mind, might stand as symbols for this small island. I stopped for a longer while at the Haunch and Venison pub, which is so small and old and British that sixteen people apologised for being in the way as I entered. I discussed prehistory (whatever that is) with Hugh and Sally, who were on a first date, before spending a happy half-hour tuning in to any one of the several conversations going on around me, as if turning the dial of a radio: a couple discussing the pros and cons of slow cookers; a trio of businessmen the likelihood of Salisbury Town's promotion.

When he first turned up in Salisbury, it was the unattractive things that caught Bryson's attention: the BKs and KFCs and Prontaprints. For me it was the attractive things: a specialist cheese shop; the general sense of goodwill and patience, notice-able as people waited for traffic lights to change or when three or four people rushed to retrieve something that had fallen from a stranger's satchel; and the maturity of the architecture, which was, to a very large extent, becoming and well-kept.

One thing that is certainly becoming and well-kept is Salisbury Cathedral. Bryson considers it the most beautiful structure in England, and its surrounding close, with its solemn houses and lawns, its most beautiful space. Sitting on a bench in the close, I contemplated the slow graft and genius and tragedy of the cathedral's construction. It was built over 40 years from 1220. The stone came from the surrounding quarries, and was transported by oxcart. There were probably some men whose entire working lives were devoted to the loading and unloading of such oxcarts, to the conveying of such stone, to the steady and laborious honouring of such a God, a God who would (surely!) reward their efforts with an easy time of it in the next life. A thousand men died raising Salisbury Cathedral.

The composer George Frideric Handel was not among them. A small notice told me that Handel would often stay in rooms just across from the cathedral, above one of the gates in the old city wall. One can imagine it being a good spot for composing; can imagine Handel looking out from his window across the close, plucking and blowing imaginary instruments, conducting thin air with loose inspired fingers. Yes, one can imagine it. But what if Handel didn't have access to such rooms, such a view, such felicitous conditions? Would his music have arisen nonetheless? Immanuel Kant, if I remember correctly, might have argued yes, that you either had it or you didn't, regardless of upbringing or level of affluence or degree of opportunity. For Kant it was mere coincidence, a fluke correlation, that those who were very good at music were those who could afford the instruments.

Of course such thinking is tosh. An artistic temperament is as likely to reside in poor and rich alike. But – and herein lies the trouble – harsh material conditions will do a good job of nullifying such a temperament, of nipping it in the bud. Is anything being done to ameliorate this? To give all young adults a fair crack of the whip? The response of recent governments to the problems of social inequality has been to suggest that such problems either don't exist, because we live in a classless society, or aren't to be worried about, because of social mobility, which allows each of us to move up and down the social ladder according to our effort and ambition, which is about as fanciful an idea as they get.

This rather bleak train of thought prompted a recent memory, of when I went to an exhibition of A-level art work at a notoriously poor further education college, whose staff had never breathed a word of Oxford or Cambridge when I was there ten years ago. Wandering the exhibition, there was an impressive discrepancy between the quality of the work and the ambitions of the artists, which were stated on accompanying cards. One boy, who had produced a fantastic piece in response to carbon emissions, wanted to pursue full-time work in retail. Another, carpentry. I don't mean to disparage or devalue such professions. Not at all. I mean to state my frustration with the far too reliable correlation between a person's socio-economic status and their aspirations and opportunities.

I got off my bench (and soapbox) and went to a Wetherspoon pub on Fisherton Street, where I sat in the window with a gin and tonic and passed some time watching people using a zebra crossing. Once they are sure that the driver has spotted them and started to slow down, they dash across apologetically, a hand raised to signal to the motorist that they really don't do this often, and wouldn't be doing it now were it not absolutely necessary. At a neighbouring table, a waitress delivered two chicken curries. The exchange lasted ten seconds; I counted seven thank yous. I genuinely do not know whether the British are a stronger or weaker people for their 'good' manners.

I thought I'd go to the cathedral for Evensong, but when I arrived the choristers were packing up their hymn sheets and saying under their breath 'Thank God that's over.' I took a pew. Twenty metres away, a well-dressed gentleman was attempting to retrieve a £20 note from a donations box. He was trying to fish it out with a distorted coat hanger. Each time a chorister or clergyman came near he would casually recoil and start whistling and checking in his pockets for change, before going back to his task. It was genuinely exciting to watch.

I had time in the morning to take a walking tour of the city before going to Stonehenge. Ordinarily, I'm not an advocate of tours of any kind. I don't like the idea that the assets of a place can be neatly ranked and built into an itinerary, which can then be prescribed, with no accounting for taste, to any one of a million visitors. Surely a place's value is the sum of those accidents and collisions and detours that are unique to each visitor: a chance conversation by the canal; the sight of a crowd of people queuing in the rain; a brave pigeon pecking your toes as you drink wine from the bottle and listen to church bells. Such things can't easily be incorporated into an itinerary. Nevertheless, I'd learnt in London that organised tours can be worthwhile, so long as you don't expect to reap from them everything that is valuable or worth knowing about a place.

At a very agreeable pace, then, Shirley showed me her city: the exposed 15th-century windows and walls of a camping store; the guildhall on Market Square, with its listed oak courtroom and extravagant banqueting hall, where Jane Austen-types would once have gone to twerk and plead not guilty; the Chapter House at the cathedral, which holds a copy of the Magna Carta; and something called the Bumping Stone, also in the cathedral, upon whose hard surface the heads of debutant choristers would once have been banged, by way of introducing them to certain metaphysical sensations, like brain damage.

Afterwards, I went to the Salisbury Museum, not to appreciate the 'diverting oddments' and scale models as Bill had, but to take coffee with Grace and Georgina, who had also taken the tour. The three of us spoke about faith and bullying and the coalition government. It was excellent talking with them. As we parted, Grace pushed a £10-note into my hand, insisting I buy myself a good dinner. She wouldn't take no for an answer, bless her cotton socks. Making my way toward the bus station, I vowed to no longer waste time mucking about with people my own age in pubs and clubs when I could be in museum cafes discussing the world with women in their sixties.

I didn't read as I waited for my bus to Amesbury (from where I would walk the few miles to Stonehenge). Instead, I just sat and watched and listened. It wasn't idleness that kept me from my book, or because I had grown bored with so-and-so's lugubrious prose. I wasn't reading my book because I was reading the bus station. I was reading its sounds and textures and traffic; its lapsed paintwork, impatient staff, out-of-order vending machine. The world, when one gets caught in this frame of mind, becomes a text, a book of the finest and longest type, full of poetry and humour and pathos and virtue and accidental beauty. And this little pocket of Salisbury, the bus station behind Blue Boar Row, just before noon at the start of winter, was for the time being my small piece of that fine and long text. I read it slowly and at length, for the bus was late.

The few miles or so that I had to walk from Amesbury to Stonehenge were along the A303. Of course there is a bus that will take you from Salisbury all the way to Stonehenge, and visitors invariably take advantage of it, but it's overpriced, and why would you pay a fiver extra when you can simply walk the last few miles?

I'll tell you why. You'd pay the fiver extra because it is eminently safer to do so. The A303 is not designed to be walked on. It is designed to convey thousands of vehicles an hour, and quickly. There was no hard shoulder or pavement, only a filament of gravel-grass between me and the stream of wing mirrors. Initially, vehicles shot past me at 60-miles-per-hour, great chains of them charging to Bristol or Yeovil or St Anthony in Roseland. But then the great chain stopped moving, and before long I was overtaking the very trucks that minutes before nearly had me in a ditch. I waved at the drivers, who were too reserved or surprised or indifferent to acknowledge me.

I could see the famous stones by now, their grey weight clear against the bottle-green grass. Up the road, I could see where the tourist buses were turning off the A303 and following a dirt track down to the carpark and ticket office. I could've followed the buses but didn't like the idea of a ticket office. Far more sensible was to hurdle the barbed wire fence, and then cut across the bottle-green field for half a mile.

Bryson lasted eleven minutes before he got bored of the stones. Of course he stayed longer, goofing about for another 40 in the visitors' centre before calling it a day. One tourist showed no such respect. He did a lap of the stones in three minutes – his iPad snapping and shooting all the while – and was back on the bus within another two, where he probably got down to the serious business of uploading his Neolithic megabytes. Being a diplomatic sort, I met the two in the middle and gave the stones seven minutes before turning on my heel.

As I walked back to Amesbury, I received a call from the Milford Hall Hotel. Apparently I owed for half a lager and some nuts.

8

Corfe Castle

In Corfe Castle, Dorset, I met up with an old friend. Charlie and I became friends at university, having bonded on our first night, when I lent the guy a pair of shoes after he had chosen to take a shortcut to the Student's Union through thick mud, rather than keep to the bitumen footpath, as anyone not from Dorset would have done. Charlie has regressed somewhat since and now works 'in TV', whatever that means. He's the sort of person that will apologise if you stand on his foot; and he chuckles when he reads the newspaper. That's all you need to know really.

When Bill arrived in Corfe Castle, he told the receptionist at Morton's House that he had that day walked all the way from Dundee, believing that the first rule of walking is to always say you've come an impossible distance. Were he younger and not covered in dung, Bryson reckons that such boasting might have earned him some romantic attention. Being younger and not covered in dung, I thought I'd test Bill's hypothesis, and so suggested to the receptionist that I too had come from Dundee, which the receptionist, Giovani from Padua, met with an invitation to sign here and here, before asking for our preferred dining time.

'8.30,' I said.

'So 8 for 8.30?'

'What?'

'If you want to eat at 8.30, come to the bar at 8 and then we'll summon you at half past.'

'Can't we just come at 8.30?'

'So you want 8.30 for 9?'

'What?'

'Come down at half-past and we'll summon you at 9.'

'So what do we do for half an hour?'

'You're encouraged to pass some time at the bar.'

'We were going to do that anyway.'

'So what's the problem?'

I took a deep breath. 'Look, how about we compromise? How about we come at 8.15?'

'So 8.15 for 8.45?'

By the time we had reached an agreement the only table left was a 9 for 9.30, which did at least give us plenty of time to smarten up. At 9.07 we went to the bar and had a pint. We asked the barman what happens in the mysterious half-hour one is asked to observe prior to dinner.

'It's just tradition,' he said.

'It used to be just tradition to hang, draw and quarter Catholics.'

'Did it?'

'Yeah.'

'In any case you can go through now.'

Dinner was worth the wait, if only for the pleasure I took in learning that the menu was as verbose as it had been two decades before. For a main, I considered the 'deep-fried duck egg in Japanese breadcrumbs, served with crushed olives and herbed potatoes, dried plum tomatoes, distressed orange coulis and a spinach salsa verde'. One doesn't know whether to eat such a thing or hang it on the wall. Also interesting was that there turned out to be a reliable correlation between the length of the dish's description and its actual size. Viz, if the description ran to more than two sentences, the dish invariably arrived in an espresso cup.

After ordering our haikus we killed some time observing our fellow diners. Close by was a table of four aristocrats. Or at least I assume they were aristocrats, on account of their saying an awful lot about awfully little in an awfully self-important way. It was all 'Oh Spain this yar was a gut-load of Charlie-Romeo-Alpha-Papa', and 'wasn't the chancellor's budget a jolly dose of Tango-Oscar-Sierra-Sierra'. In fact, I can only be sure that two of the party were aristocratic, for the other two said nothing at all. They just got on with eating their solar-powered plum tomatoes, dutifully taking on the chin all the Tango-Oscar-Sierra-Sierra being offered by their dining partners.

It was bonfire night and so after dinner we went to the Greyhound Inn to watch a display of fireworks. The pub garden was rammed, which didn't surprise me, as given half the chance, the British will consistently and willingly attend underwhelming events. To be fair, the display in question deserved the collective 'ooohs' and 'aaahs' issued by the crowd. Each explosion gave a brief floodlight onto the ruined castle, whose fallen rampart or sunken keep was of a sudden pink or green or orange.

After the fireworks we went to the Fox Inn, having been told by several people over the previous hour not to. At the pub's entrance, we peered in sheepishly. A man sat alone at a table, a great tuft of chest hair escaping his shirt and a great tuft of nose escaping his face. He beckoned us to join him. His name was John and over the next hour he didn't so much talk with us as offer occasional, unpublishable grunts, about the various drugs he'd been smoking, about Jimi Hendrix, about local councillors. At one point, John was kind enough to take us outside to smoke something he called 'pollen', which I think was hashish. A woman walked past. John stared at the ground as she passed and then watched her intently as she walked into the distance. 'I used to mean a lot to her,' he said.

John moved on to another pub and we went back inside. The only other party present, relieved by John's exit, were now talking boisterously. They were clearly interested in Charlie and me. Not often, I imagine, do two unknown young men willingly chew the fat with John. I asked one of the group – a haughty woman of pensionable age – whether the village had changed much over the years. 'Yes of course, Fred!' (She immediately and inexplicably took to calling me Fred.) 'The people are older!' I asked if there had been much immigration. 'Yes, Fred! Rich people!' It was the woman's opinion that of all types of immigrant, rich people were generally the worst, as they push people out of properties that they then don't bother to use, save for occasional weekends.

The woman's friends had other ideas, however. For them the biggest problem was the East Europeans, who drank and smoked on street corners and generally caused a nuisance. I said – throwing in my tuppence worth – that the people who emigrate to Britain tend to be the least advantaged from their native country, people looking for work and better living conditions, and so it's perhaps not surprising that a small number of them do such things – things, I was ready to point out, that plenty of British men and women do. And I asked them – as gently and reasonably as possible – to retain their opinions but to remember that the East Europeans have to make a living and relax and socialise as any other people, and that for every one who is behaving in a less-than-refined way, fifteen more are cooking or cleaning or catching a bus or putting their children to bed or watching the news or seeing to the garden or writing worried letters back to lonesome grandparents. They called for another bottle of wine and two extra glasses.

After a good night's sleep, we took breakfast in the dining room, having been summoned four days earlier. That done, we set off to pick up the coast path. At Kingston, which sits on high ground, we turned to consider the view of Corfe Castle in its low gap between two hills, burnished by the sometime shining sun. We read aloud Bill's description of the view. It was an odd sensation. It somehow felt – although plainly not the case – that Bryson was just metres or miles ahead, and that we were somehow in his wake, happily stalking behind. Perhaps it was the fidelity between his description and what we saw before us that made him seem close. Elsewhere on this trip, on high streets and at train stations, there had been obvious differences between what Bill had written and what I had encountered. On such occasions, it was easy to feel displaced from the source material and its author. But when there was nothing separating the then and the now, the twenty years contract and Bill's footsteps seemed just a dozen paces off.

We spent a couple of hours after Kingston trying haplessly to get back to the coast path, passing through fields of cattle and forgotten machinery. I said to Charlie that this kind of walk was as much an audio as a visual experience, drawing his attention to the sound of the wind and the cattle (and the cattle's wind) and the distant sea and traffic, and said that talk of there being no room on this island for more people seemed absurd amid all this space, and anyway what are all these fields for, Charlie, because they don't seem at all farmable, and did you ever read what Wordsworth had to say about the city polluting the soul, and don't you think that travelling is like meditation because the mind is totally engaged with fresh phenomena – scenes, smells, sounds – with the result that it becomes impossible to dwell on our favourite anxieties, like money or relationships or our appearance or the future, and might that be why I feel so much happier now than a few weeks ago, Charlie?

At Swyre Head – one end of a tall inland ridge – I looked at the hills to the west, and Sandbanks and Bournemouth and the Isle of Wight to the east, and Corfe Castle to the north, and the endless sea to the south. I had never seen so much while stood on a natural platform. I felt small, yes, and humble, yes, but at the same time I felt more meaningful and alive, ready to yelp or whistle or embrace someone, ready to phone loved ones and tell them exactly why they were loved, ready to stop strangers in their tracks and tell them they're bright and unique, ready to kiss Charlie full on the lips. Charlie looked up from his map; looked at me. Was he feeling the same way? Was he ready for the same things? 'I think it's this way,' he said.

This stretch of the coastal path hugs the Jurassic Coast, a World Heritage site that has been voted by *Radio Times* readers – and who is to argue with them? – the fifth-greatest natural wonder of Britain. I'm not sure how, but apparently the Jurassic Coast contrives to document 180 million years of geological history (something to do with dead seagulls?). As it does so, the coastline climbs and falls. Most of the hills are no more than a few hundred feet high, but are often very steep. Accordingly, after only an hour's walking Bryson had worked up quite a thirst. Taking advantage of his binoculars, Bryson scanned the horizon, whereupon he spotted his salvation – a Portakabin next to Kimmeridge Bay, which he hoped was a tearoom or similar, but which turned out to be a National Trust recruitment site. Luckily, an ice cream van turned up, from which Bill was able to purchase six bottles of Panda Cola, which he greedily imbibed, but which proved – lo and behold – oddly unsatisfying.

As Charlie and I descended into Kimmeridge, I hoped there would be no such van, and no such cola, because after the English breakfast I'd had that morning I shouldn't have thought introducing a litre of pop into my system would do me any favours. In any case, there was no van, and so we bundled past the grotesque rockery that characterises the small bay here, and then onwards until we reached Osmington Beach, where we picnicked on pork pies and Mars bars, and watched a cormorant bear over and then filch a far better lunch than ours.

A mile or so further on we came to Tyneham. The Ministry of Defence still used this part of the coast to test out its new gear. No one lives here of course, but they once did. The erstwhile residents of Tyneham were evacuated during the Second World War so the army could run military drills. The residents were never resettled, which must have been a real pain, particularly, Bill points out, for 'those who forgot to cancel their milk'. Bill regrets that the Army continue to practise here, when they could actually offer a service to the nation by doing so in Keighley, Yorkshire. Personally, I regret that they continue to practise anywhere at all.

We were losing light and West Lulworth – where we were due to stay the night – was still some way off, despite a man telling us a few hours earlier that it was just around the corner. On account of the man's counsel, we'd taken a longer lunch break and adopted a less hurried pace, so now here we were scrambling desperately up and down Bindon Hill, in a race with the encroaching dusk.

The toil was certainly getting to Charlie, who by this point was issuing no more than the occasional grunt or sigh; and by the time we had finally begun our descent into West Lulworth, he had stopped making any noise at all. This didn't worry me unduly. After eight hours in a man's company, those moments when you forget you're with them are not altogether unpleasant. To console Charlie, I told him that his present struggle had a precedent; that Chapter Eight concludes with Bill frothing from the mouth and delirious, his body a cheap imitation of what it was earlier that day.

'But Bill had something to look forward to,' said Charlie. 'In Bryson's mind, Lulworth was the quintessential postcard seaside resort, rivalled only by St Tropez. And so he pushed on eagerly. I, however, having read Chapter Nine, know that Lulworth is actually rather crap.'

9

West Lulworth–Weymouth

West Lulworth isn't actually rather crap. It wasn't then and it isn't now. One of its several virtues is certainly the Lulworth Cove Inn, where Charlie and I had agreed to meet his father, who, having been spared the taxing tramp from Corfe Castle, seemed to have gained twenty years on us. He might have passed as a teenager next to Charlie and I, with our wind-beaten faces and crooked postures and spoilt forms.

It was certainly Charlie's father who was in the most youthful mood. As the three of us waited on roast beef, he began to recite a poem he had written about the nearby Isle of Portland. Charlie nipped the recital in the bud after four metric feet, raising a cautionary hand in his father's direction and saying, 'Dad. No.'

After dinner, father and son went off to the former's home ten miles away. I was staying in a room above the pub, having enquired between courses whether the management were at all keen to put me up at a friendly rate, on account of a book I probably wouldn't finish. At first the staff member dealing with me had looked suspicious, and so I did what I normally do in such situations, which is to say I got out my bruised and much-annotated copy of Bryson's text and flopped it down onto the counter (as if to confirm just how seriously I take these things), before pretending to receive a phone call in which I made a point of saying such things as 'If you forward the invoice,

Stanley, I'll see to it in the fullness of time.' My performance did the trick: a friendly room rate came forth.

I was shown to a room whose decor and arrangement were of the shabby-chic genre of interior design, which, as far as I can tell, involves having the bathtub outside of the bathroom, no carpets or wallpaper, and a general look of near-completion. As with my room in Windsor, it was far more stylish than I could ever hope to be. Accordingly, I was reluctant to leave it.

I was also reluctant to leave it because Bryson's night in Lulworth hadn't been the best. The reason Bryson had a disappointing night was mostly due to the fact that he had arrived in Lulworth with such high hopes; hopes that had been fabricated by a collection of Ladybird children's books, which portrayed the British seaside as a place where the sun always shone, the shopkeepers always smiled, and the children did nothing more daring or improper than sail model boats or catch crabs.

What's more, Bryson also remembered Lulworth to be such an idyllic place, having visited with his family some years before. But memory, as children's books, is prone to gloss over the negative elements of an experience and dwell instead on the positive things, like fresh seafood and long afternoons under the covers while the kids were busy drowning somewhere. In short, holidays tend to be better after the fact.

In the event, I had a pretty nice time staying in, if you don't mind me saying. I made some notes about the day's walking at my distressed-driftwood bureau, and then watched *Question Time* in the bath, whence I learned that the people of High Wycombe would like lower taxes and better public services, thank you very much.

In the morning the sun was shining, so there was no need for me to do as Bill had done and spend half an hour struggling into a pair of waterproofs until I resembled a large blue condom. This was probably just as well, given that Charlie is a Catholic.

Making quick progress past Durdle Door and Hambury Tout, I noticed the grass more than anything, darting and shifting in the warm wind, as if trying to lose its green, or prise itself from the earth. There is fun to be had kicking such grass, as there is fun to be had doing anything for no reason. If one acts with a reason, one is liable to be anxious of the outcome throughout the doing. If one acts without a reason, there can be no anxiety, and one's actions take on a lightness and innocence, and can only be good.

I would have liked to kick the cliffs as well. They were white and puffy like a type of goat's cheese, and seemed to invite hungry abseilers, who would lower themselves into their creamy face and build sandwiches from their historic strata. Inland a few metres, a society of cows, whose milk might once have given form to the cliffs, took elevenses on the crest of a steep-sided hill called Scratchy Bottom, which, quite like when someone yawns and you copy, compelled me to scratch my own as I passed it.

The view doesn't change a great deal along this stretch of the coast – not appreciably, anyhow. As a result, one is less attentive to it. As with a clock, or a painting, or a building whose appearance is apparently steady, one initial gulp of looking feels sufficient. There is no need to fix our gaze to it, for we are confident it promises little alteration. So it was with the scenery as we continued onwards to Weymouth, which became little more than a situation for our walking, a passive context through which we had to pass if we were to reach our destination. No doubt I was doing the scene a huge disservice by adopting this attitude, and betraying a lack of sensitivity, but that's how it was.

Things changed as we lowered into the outskirts of Weymouth. Behind me a rainbow was cutting across the bronze cliff face. I could have done with a pair of wing mirrors, so often did I turn to see the dying rainbow against the burnished cliff. At this end of Weymouth's long curving beach sat a slumbering amusement park and a low, art deco mansion, while down on the beach a great quantity of shingle was being repositioned by bright glowing machines. And in a fit of roundabout totalitarianism a sign politely warned: 'I AM VERY SORRY BUT NO VESSELS ARE TO BE LAUNCHED HERE OR HEREABOUTS'.

To mark his special relationship with the town, the chalk hillside nearby has a carving of George III riding a horse. Significantly, George was depicted riding away from Weymouth, which the king interpreted as a jibe at his expense, a hint that the locals wouldn't mind one bit if his royal highness trotted off for a while. The man responsible for the carving killed himself when he learnt of the king's upset.

More interesting, to my mind, is why George chose to holiday in Weymouth so much in the first place – fourteen times between 1789 and 1805, which seems an unlikely enthusiasm. Why didn't he visit France now and again? Not only is the food and weather generally better there, but George could have dropped in on his second cousin, Louis XIV, who, having recently lost his job, could no doubt have done with some cheering up.

We checked in at the Royal Hotel. We were given separate rooms: the Superior and the Premier. We couldn't decide which was supposed to be better than the other so tossed for it and spent the next hour or so as we unpacked and assimilated calling each other on the internal phone network, asking such questions as 'How big are your cups?' and 'Did you get nail-clippers?' In fact, the rooms were more or less identical, though Charlie's bathtub was a foot or so shorter than mine, which was unfortunate, given that he's a foot or so longer than me.

After taking tea in the bay window of Premier (or was it Superior?) we left the hotel and went looking for a restaurant called Perry's, where Bryson had a 'highly creditable sea bass'. The restaurant is now called Oasis and under different management, but continues to dish out excellent food. I ate a starter of local mackerel which was big enough to be a main course, and then a main of pork belly with black pudding that was small enough to be a starter. Interestingly, the waitress was 'glad' about everything. I mentioned to her that we were walking the coastal path: she was glad about that. I mentioned the favourable size of the starter: she was glad about that also. I was tempted, as we settled the bill, to tell her that when it comes to the Premier and Superior rooms at the Royal Hotel a feather would tip the scales, to see if she was glad about that too. Lovely really, on reflection, to have met someone so glad.

Keen to follow Bill's example of getting drunk enough that his feet no longer ached, we went first to The Stable, where they offer 50 types of cider and serve pizzas with postmodern toppings, and then to The Ship a few doors down, where I had the feeling that the owners had gone a little overboard (if you will) on the nautical design scheme.

Generally speaking, Weymouth was looking quite spruce, and I wondered whether the town – a sailing hotspot – had spent a chunk of money improving itself in the run up the 2012 Olympics. Earlier, when checking into the hotel, I had suggested to the receptionist that the summer of 2012 must have been very lucrative for the area. The receptionist assured me that if anything the opposite was the case, explaining how the local council's apocalyptic warnings of traffic congestion and insistence that all visitors park a long way outside of Weymouth (Dundee, for example) and then walk in, ensured that the hotel, and Weymouth generally, had its quietest summer for years. Many local businesses, anticipating a bumper summer, were left out of pocket, and many councillors, I hope, were carved into the chalk hills riding away from the city.

We had a couple of nightcaps at a place called Rendezvous, where we caught the attention of a middle-aged woman called Juliette, who accused Charlie and I of being a rich gay couple in town to buy up property. We said that rich gay couples don't drink £1.50 whisky and cokes. Unconvinced, she asked what we did for a living. I said I lived off Charlie, who presented the weather on Channel 5. She leaned in drunkenly, told me in no uncertain terms that Charlie wasn't her type, and then went to the dance floor to snog a substantial bald man, who obviously was. It was a rather strange five minutes.

We wandered home through Weymouth's small warren of shopping streets, noting the Fantastic Sausage Factory and The Cheapest Charity Shop in Dorset, and the once modern and busy cinema complex, which can no longer afford to employ someone to hawk popcorn. I wanted to head away from the postcard district and out into the residential streets, to gain a more complete sense of the town. After all, a place is the sum of its parts – its housing estates and industrial parks as well as its esplanade and harbourside. But it was too late and I was too drunk. If I'd ventured deep into Weymouth's underbelly there was a chance I'd have fallen in with the wrong crowd and settled there.

We were the last guests to return to the hotel. The night porter was anxious to start vacuuming. Charlie and I went our separate ways, he to Superior, I to Premier. In a bid to sober up, I passed some time watching Michael Portillo in a pink blazer riding trains on BBC2, passing out as he approached Eccles. Then the phone rang. It was Charlie. Was he sore about Juliette? Did he want to ask – at long, long last – if it wouldn't be the worst thing in the world if we *were* a rich gay couple in town to buy property? I picked up the receiver and waited for Charlie to speak. 'Ben. I can't sleep without asking.' I held my breath. 'What brand are your biscuits?'

When Charlie's breakfast arrived, I was pleased to note – in keeping with his Superior status – a shorter sausage. I looked out at the dismal morning weather: banks of espresso-cloud gave gusts of shrapnel rain, while the bay was a disco of scalene triangles. The waitress arrived with extra beans.

'It's clearing up nicely,' she said.

'Is it?'

'Well, you never know.'

A lot has been written about the relationship between walking and thinking. Perhaps unsurprisingly, for one is often mother to the other. Put one way, the act of walking is straight-forward enough to let the mind walk also. What's more, the speed at which walking typically happens allows the walker to casually consume and digest the passing slideshow – pheasant tracks, bench carvings, a discarded scooter, the clouds – all of which is fodder to the imagination. The exposing quality of walking makes it a handmaiden to thought; but the exposing quality of walking also pits the walker against the elements, i.e. shrapnel rain shot from espresso-cloud. All of which is a roundabout way of saying we chose not to walk to Chesil Beach but to take the bus instead.

A lot has also been written about the peculiar pebbles of Chesil Beach – that start as peas and finish as plums, shrinking from west to east with each lap of the surf – so I'll mention only the ambitious seagulls who, for twenty minutes at a time, drove their bills into the teeth of that afternoon's breeze, going nowhere on windy treadmills. Inspired by the endeavour of the gulls (and the rain having eased), we continued westward on foot.

Over the years, the shingle of Chesil Beach has been forced backward into a high bank, rendering the sea invisible from the slightly inland coast path. As a result, this section of the coastal path is often interpreted – as it was by Bryson – as the 'most boring' imaginable.

But for us it was a happy course, for we knew that at the end of it was a late lunch at West Bay's Riverside Cafe, one of the most coveted seafood restaurants in the south, a slice of Ralph Lauren Chelsea on the Dorset coast. Bryson took an extravagant lunch at the Riverside Cafe, diving into a lobster and scallop terrine, a bottle of Chardonnay, and yet another fillet of sea bass – this one 'exquisite' rather than 'highly creditable', suggesting that Bryson understands the benefits of a diverse diet.

About an hour out from the restaurant we got a text message from the mother of Charlie's ex-girlfriend, which carried the information that the restaurant stopped serving lunch in half an hour. It strikes me as an overreaction now, but we genuinely panicked. Charlie spotted a car parked close by. I knocked on its window. The driver, after brief consultation with his passenger, lowered it. I said we were experiencing a bit of an emergency and needed to be in West Bay as soon as possible. The driver, again after brief consultation with his passenger, unlocked the back doors, bade me get the hell in, then raced off into the afternoon, leaving Charlie stranded in the carpark. When I brought this last point to his attention, he cursed softly, somehow reversed in fifth gear, gathered my companion, then raced off once more into the ever-so-slightly-later afternoon.

With his foot to the floor, Mick told us everything we needed to know: that he was ex-SAS, that he knew the Riverside Cafe well, that he understood our predicament perfectly, that he recommended the mushy peas. We reached West Bay in record time, climbed out gloriously, swapped dog tags with Mick, hastened to the restaurant and its promise of fresh fish in a well-to-do atmosphere.

It was closed.

Our disappointment was soundtracked by the prolonged chord of Mick's horn. We turned around. Mick, stung by the failure, by the botched mission, had his head pressed against the steering wheel. It was all I could do not to fall to my knees and roar to the uncaring sky. Charlie drew closer; put his hand on my shoulder. Was *this* the moment that would bring us together? Had it taken tragedy to loosen Charlie's innermost tongue? 'Do you think Mick can drop us at KFC?'

10

Exeter–Barnstaple

Mick didn't drop us at KFC. Instead, we lunched on a cone of chips from a wooden kiosk whose proprietor resembled the actor Timothy Spall. In Timothy's opinion, just about everything in West Bay was too new – the pier, the local teenagers, even the Jurassic Coast itself. I told him that things can't help but change. 'Yeah, well, they should change back again.'

I wanted to mention John Boynton Priestley, who back in 1933 during his *English Journey*, grew tired of this type of knee-jerk nostalgia, of those people 'who believe that in some mysterious way we can all return to this Old England' but say nothing of 'killing off nine-tenths of our present population, which would have to be the first step'.

One thing Timothy doesn't consider too new is Margaret, who's been selling ice cream from a neighbouring kiosk for 164 years. Margaret pulled me an ice cream then poured Charlie a cup of tea, complaining vociferously as she did so about the new pier and the new teenagers and even Timothy Spall, who she considers too new by half.

The ice cream machine that Margaret uses is plainly a relic of the Boer War, and the same might be said of her husband, whose contribution to the local economy is limited, as far as I can tell, to staring accusingly at the new pier and the new teenagers and nodding energetically each time Margaret wants something confirmed.

Having had his chips and his cup of tea, and his bracing hike along the coast, Charlie turned inland and set off for London. I, on the other hand, was kindly gathered and put up for the night by the mother of Charlie's ex-girlfriend (who the day before, if you remember, had delivered the bad news regarding the Riverside's opening hours).

Yvonne treated me ever so well, forcing a bowl of chilli and a glass of mulled wine on me within minutes of admitting me to her house. We watched the news together and discussed various things, but mostly her daughter Sophie, who on account of her general brilliance deserves to have been the principal topic of conversation in every living room that evening.

After retiring to the guest bedroom and conceding to the thick darkness particular to the countryside, I woke up a certain time later requiring the toilet. Returning from said toilet, I became confused by the dark and the novelty of the house, and very nearly got into bed with my hostess. I wonder to this day how far Yvonne's hospitality might have extended.

In the morning, Yvonne gave me a lift into the small market town of Bridport, famous for its rope and New Year's Eve parties. At the latter, the younger members of the community (that is, all those under 70) dress up as prehistoric fossils and B-list celebrities, with the most interestingly dressed person winning a minibreak to West Bay. Perhaps Timothy Spall wins the event every year, which is why he's always down the bay flogging chips.

After some idle poking about in Bridport, I strolled the short distance to West Bay to have a belated lunch at the Riverside. On top of my lunch, I also had a friendly conversation with the restaurant's proprietor, Arthur Watson, who was at the helm when Bryson visited twenty years ago. Watson remembers the occasion, and even encouraged me to sit where Bill had. Bryson didn't ask anything about the restaurant at the time of his visit, said Watson, but called a few months later when he was writing up the chapter with a list of questions, two of which were, '*How* much did I eat?' and 'What do you mean I didn't leave a tip?'

After polishing off a red mullet, I bade farewell to Arthur and clambered aboard the X53 bus, a recently introduced service that stalks the coast all the way to Exeter. And what a service it is. West of Bridport, the flanking hills were a confused assembly of snooker tables, meeting to discuss the depth of their pockets. At Charmouth, paint only comes in tins of blue and lemon and pink – the colours of Venice or St Petersburg. At Lyme Regis, where the bus had to slalom skilfully to avoid hanging baskets, the shops – Rummage, Ruby Rockcake, The Ginger, Serendip – suggest ice cream flavours.

And at the end of it all was Exeter, on whose eastern edge squats a portion of the university campus, dead opposite the police station, which is a prudent proximity if ever there was one. Even out here on the edge, the city is a confusion of old and new, and I wondered, as the bus leaked into the centre, how good Exeter would have looked had it not been bombed so heavily during the Second World War, for the buildings that survived the Luftwaffe are some of the prettiest I've seen.

One such building is The Royal Clarence hotel, where Bill stayed the night. I went to the hotel now, knocked the assistant manager down to £50 including breakfast, deposited my bag, and returned to the streets in possession of a single objective, inherited from Bryson: to find a Chinese restaurant and then make a mess of the table.

But one has to ready oneself for such things, and so first I went to the Wetherspoon pub on South Street, formerly a Unitarian Church, where I had a Guinness and surveyed the crowd to get a sense of Exeter's demographic, and maybe identify one or two parties who wouldn't be averse to my company. I approached a group of labourers with a classic icebreaker – 'Pardon me, but what do you guys think of the X53?' – which failed to elicit the invitation I was hoping for.

I quit the pub and turned right, stopping at the junction of North and South Streets, where a market was busy selling fresh fish, bread, beetroot, game and Devonshire cheese. I asked myself why these artisans had been forced out onto the street, had been made a travelling circus of once-a-week mongers and grocers, their former high-street homes given over to salons and nail bars and pound-stores.

My next stop was St Pancras Church, which, for better or worse, is enveloped by a 1980s shopping centre. Inside the church, small handwritten messages to God (tweets almost) were pinned to a corkboard: a boy wishing for a seventeen-inch flatscreen TV; a man for a holiday in Cyprus; a girl for her mother to be cured of Lupus.

Along from the church, on Fore Street, a scattering of grand old buildings are put to pedestrian uses: fried chicken, stationery, hairdressing. Unlike Salisbury's ancient buildings, which are everywhere and thus easy to take for granted, Exeter's seem to pop out from amid post-war mistakes and are more impressive and arresting as a result, for it is change that catches our attention, not continuity, no matter how pleasant the constant thing.

Keen to postpone my Chinese dinner yet further, I went to a pub on John Street called The Fat Pig, whose ales are brewed upstairs and have won medals. I went through to the garden and there found and read a book on sociology (voting patterns in Rochdale), before falling in with a musician-baker called Jimmy, and his pal Tom, who lives on a barge and is researching reverse engineered silk, be that what it may. Jimmy and Tom took me to The Hour Glass, where we drank neat gin that tasted of lemon and juniper and evoked the novels of George Orwell.

The Royal Clarence disapproved as I ignored its warmth and walked further into the night, passing several Chinese restaurants that I couldn't bring myself to enter, having no urge by this time to spend a solitary hour eating prawn crackers and reflecting, as Bill had, on how a people that invented gunpowder and paper and sweet-and-sour chicken balls could still think it sensible to grasp food with knitting needles.

But it wasn't just Chinese I was avoiding. It was most things. It was as many things as possible. All I wanted was to keep walking – under lamplight, under moonlight, around Exeter – until the melancholy passed.

I ate breakfast in the window of the Clarence's dining room, overlooking the Cathedral Close. The latter really is a fine space, offering a range of architectural styles, each suggesting a different country or epoch or ideology, so that the complete close teems with various associations: dinners in Paris, picnics in Gent, arguments in London. What's more, the relative modesty of the enclosing buildings exaggerates the visual impact of the centrally located cathedral. The total composition is really quite something.

After breakfast, I went to Marks & Spencer to buy a pastry I didn't want and look at the women fussing with coins and receipts. Bryson, you see, didn't breakfast at the Clarence. Instead, he opted to buy a pastry from Marks & Spencer so he could study the women in line there. Bryson liked how the women – when they finally got to the front of the line – would act surprised that they actually had to pay for something, and then spend countless minutes digging for the correct change in their handbags, to the obvious chagrin of the lady next in queue, who in a few moments would do exactly the same thing.

Nineteen years later, nobody was paying with cash. Instead, creditable plastic plunged into endless payment slots. From what I could tell, the women before me were handling this contemporary way of purchasing with dexterity. It was the men that seemed incompetent, first struggling to find their wallet, then struggling to find the correct card, then struggling to ascertain which end of the card went in which end of the machine, then struggling to recall their PIN, which used to be the birthday of their eldest but God knows what it is now. And there was also the added spectacle of contactless payment, which never seemed to effect a swift transaction. Again it was the men that struggled, slapping and smothering their card on the beckoning screen for up to five minutes, in which time the women had driven home and put a quiche in the oven.

Then I went to Barnstaple for a tuna sandwich. I would rather have a debilitating condition than eat tuna, and I don't particularly like Barnstaple, but Bryson had a tuna sandwich in Barnstaple and so I would as well.

As the train rattled north from Exeter, my anxiety regarding the sandwich was compounded by a keen sense of the general pointlessness of the journey. You see, Bryson went to Barnstaple with a view to finding a connecting bus to Minehead, which proved impossible, and so was left with little option but to return to Exeter an hour later and start all over again. So here I was taking a three-hour round trip just to have a sandwich that I really didn't want. Oh, the edifying thrills of mimicry.

I walked from the station into town and found the hotel where Bill had his sandwich – The Royal and Fortescue – without ado. It was full of serious-seeming people discussing winter fuel allowances and how little they could reasonably bequeath to their children.

I ordered a tuna sandwich with so little enthusiasm that the waitress actually asked me if I was sure. When it came, the sandwich was cut into triangles, no doubt in an effort to make it seem less hostile. I managed two or three bites before pathetically attempting to hide the remainder beneath a charmless side salad.

I paid the £6.75, tipped the waitress a quid, then got the hell out of there, feeling really quite perturbed. As I crossed the fine wide bridge that connects Barnstaple with its station, I considered throwing myself from it, certain that the cold, brown, quickly-flowing water would be preferable to the solid world of trains and streets and tuna sandwiches.

Then I remembered that I had a room booked for that night in a two-star hotel in Weston-super-Mare, and so kept right on walking.

11

Weston-super-Mare–Monmouth

In the Quiet Zone of the 18.40 to Weston-super-Mare, I did as Bill had done – I reflected on the small matter of existence and whether we ought to be grateful for getting a go at it.

In short, I feel no obligation to be happy for being alive. I didn't ask for the opportunity. I wasn't alive for millions of years and it was fine. And no doubt being dead will be pretty stress-free as well, for as far as I know when you're dead other people don't die, or get really ill, and the person you're crazy in love with doesn't gradually and dishonestly grow less attracted to you. No, *life* is the problematic period. Granted, I'm not sufficiently discontent to pull the plug early, but nor have I much time for invitations (like Bill's) to be constantly delighted just because I chanced to be in the right batch of spermatozoa.

One thing that is unlikely to make anybody happy is finding themselves alone in Weston-super-Mare on a rainy Tuesday evening in November. There was not a soul on the platform when I alighted, an atmosphere at odds with the one that had presided on the train, whose designated Quiet Zone had proved anything but. Case in point: between Taunton and Bridgwater a group of teenagers discussed loudly the likelihood that each had a sexually transmitted infection.

I made my way to the seafront, knowing that my hotel was thereabouts. In a Caffè Nero, one of nineteen on the high street, I asked the barista if she was happy in Weston. She waited for the grinder to quiet, then said: 'You go to Bristol for stuff like that.'

And I could well believe her, for about me were signs of desolation and disquiet. As in Weymouth, Weston's founding concern was domestic tourism, made possible by the Victorian railways. But what trains gaveth, planes tooketh, and now tourism limps along stoically.

To its credit, the local council is doing its best to prop the place up: the sculpture, Silica – part kiosk, bus shelter and artwork – was meant to represent man's harmony with the sea, but has been for the most part dismissed as an expensive carrot; £38 million has been spent making it harder to fall over on the promenade; £50 million has been spent on an indoor skydiving facility; and in a cavalier move to reclaim business from Ryanair, there is even talk of a helicopter museum.

When I arrived at The Seaward, Sharon on reception greeted me like an errant son that owed her money. 'This the Bob Bryson book you were on about, is it?' Sharon asked, taking it from me and then doing that thing that all people do when discussing a book they've no idea about, which is to look at both covers and then flick aimlessly through the pages, as if by assessing the font and pagination they might gain an impression of the book's style and overriding concerns.

'Is it just you, then?' asked Sharon.

'For the moment.'

'What do you mean for the—'

'I mean who knows who I'll bump into.'

'I don't fancy your chances.'

'That's pessimistic.'

'Not in November. People don't come out till March.'

'Can't you hurry them up?'

'And then only if there's a deal on at The Duck and Ballsack.'

'The where?'

'So what did Bob Bryson do 'ere then?'

'Not much. A Chinese meal, some time in an amusement arcade, got wet, got locked out, accused his landlady of not being the most charming person he'd ever met.'

'Well I dare say you'll manage most of that.'

'That's good.'

'Did we say 10 per cent off?'

'Fifty.'

'Christ. I must have been pissed.'

I liked my room. As far as I can tell, each star that a hotel can boast of corresponds to a certain amount of pointless stuff in the rooms. If nothing else, two-star rooms are certainly manageable. So it was with room 17 at The Seaward. There was nothing on the bed to take off before I could get in. There was no vanity pack to get confused by. And, best of all, there was no distracting view because there was no window.

Following Bryson's example, I went to the Dragon Kiss Chinese Buffet on Queen Street, where George Michael was playing on a radio and a Spanish football match was being shown on an old Casio television. The decor was noisy – inconsistent lighting, hyperactive fruit machines – and there were no chopsticks, a sure sign that the local Chinese don't put a foot inside the place. I sampled four types of meat in different neon sauces before resorting to a plate of chips and a bowl of strawberry ice cream.

After Dragon Kiss, I walked The Boulevard and its tributaries until I happened upon a bar screening a Quentin Tarantino film. I took a double vodka and caught the final twenty minutes, wherein 87 per cent of the cast came to a sudden end, which did nothing for my mood, I can tell you. I left as the credits ran, and would have lingered outside to sob my heart out had my attention not been caught by a bar in the near-distance called Cheers, which I entered ironically, sensing that the place might just about finish me off. There were perhaps half a dozen people inside, and to be fair they all seemed pretty cheery. I got talking to one chap who told me that Weston was the best place in the world. Now there's a glass-half-full kind of guy if ever there was one.

Unlike Bryson, when I got back to my hotel I hadn't been locked out. It wasn't so much the being locked out that bothered Bill, more that he happened to be soaking wet at the time, having just been drenched by a passing Fiesta. When the proprietor of the hotel finally emerged to admit his guest, Bill employed some 'immoderate language' to convey the opinion that locking out guests who'd recently been ill enough to watch *This Morning* with Richard and Judy for longer than twenty minutes was just not cricket. In apology, the proprietor fetched Bill a tray of sandwiches. Bill wasn't best pleased with the offering – 'I don't want anything but to go to my room and count the minutes until I get out of this fucking dump!' – but accepted them nonetheless.

In the morning I went to have a look at the Grand Pier, reopened in 2008 following a fire. The pier has certainly suffered a thorough renovation – its signage, decor and amusements are now, I'm afraid to say, of the cheapest and most obvious sort.

I continued along the promenade until a quirky souvenir shop stopped me in my tracks. The owner of the shop – a man in his eighties or so – took this as a cue to put the kettle on. 'You'll have a cup, I presume?' he said.

Over the course of that cup of tea, Cliff told me the following: that many people think the new pier is too noisy but he just turns his hearing aid off; that the tide here is the second fastest in the world, or it might be third; and that it's a shame Portsmouth has lost its shipbuilding to Glasgow, which he suspects to be an effort to squash the Scottish independence movement. I asked Cliff if he was happy in Weston. 'What more do you want? You can see Wales from here.'

And you could see Wales, and so I went there, but not before a 50-minute wait for a connecting train to Chepstow at Severn Tunnel Junction, which must be the most singular station in the country.

It is somehow otherworldly – that is to say, it is of a world where train stations have been reduced to their bare function, which is to provide a place for a person to stand and a train to stop. Even those things that one might expect to be useful for a station's longevity – a ticket office, some passengers – are thought beside the point here.

Owing to the general absence of things, what remained took on more meaning and appeal. I considered the construction of the footbridge; the means by which the platform signs were suspended; the yellow bins of gritting salt; the seeming unsuitability of the slim tracks to steer and propel a twelve-carriage train; the underside of such a train, where there hangs a baffling consortium of hopefully effective mud-coloured pistons and rivets and panels and God knows what else.

Curious to know what the town of Severn Tunnel Junction was like, I walked for some minutes away from the station, but could only find an untended allotment and a forgotten hotel. All in all, J.G. Ballard couldn't conjure a more disconcerting environment. When you finally take your train and arrive at Chepstow, it's as if you've pulled into Penn Station, New York. Boy, did I need a pint.

So I had one, at the Chepstow Castle Inn, where a five year old dropped in after school to play the piano. I didn't stick around long, because I had to find a connecting bus to Monmouth, which I did, the 69. As the bus wound through the Wye Valley, my attention was held by a man with a moustache the size of a banana, who was telling two ladies about an immigrant who got £10,000 from the government to become a pilot for British Airways. The moustache then mentioned his nephew who had graduated from Bristol University but couldn't even get an interview at Greggs the Baker. 'They reckon he'll jump ship when something better comes up,' he explained. 'But it might never. He's paid top money and now he's in a worse position than before. There's something up with that.' The ladies reasoned that Greggs the Baker was very well-priced though.

After the winding 69, I took another bus up the hill to Penallt, where I had reserved a room at the inn. I won't afford much space to what happened at said inn, for I fear it would be a touch boastful to mention at any length the caramelised pear and roasted duck and bread-and-butter pudding that I ate for dinner, or that you could stop a door with a slice of the morning bacon, or that the black pudding had that soft maroon interior that I like so much. No, I will mention only my thoughts on the Welsh weather: awful but due to clear up nicely.

Monmouth is an old market town of roughly 9,000 residents that grew around the confluence of the Wye and Monnow rivers. It is within two miles of England, which is about the only thing that spoils it. Bryson certainly liked the place, considering Monmouth a 'fine, handsome town with a sloping High Street and an imposing town hall'. As per his custom, he didn't do much to test this opinion. He took a look at the statue of Charles Stewart Rolls, pioneer of dangerous ways to spend an afternoon, before spending the next six pages promoting the Monmouth Bookshop on Church Street, for no other reason than it had a book of his in the window.

To be fair, Bryson also found time to buy a Cornish pasty. I tried to do the same at the Waitrose deli counter, but was held up by the bald gentleman before me, who thought it smart to field several phone calls while ordering cuts of ham. I waited patiently for ten minutes before (in my dreams) pushing in front and asking the butcher to take two thick slices off this guy's shiny pate and then charge him 30 quid a kilo should he want them back.

I took my pasty to the River Wye and, drawn on by its swift brown flow, headed briefly to England. Sometimes the river appeared to idle or tarry, as if hesitant to hit the border. At other times it appeared to go past in a hurry, late for a meeting with the Thames. Beneath my soles, orange leaves gave up their final crunch. About me, the yellows and browns and reds gathered so tightly, so uniformly, that I had never felt as bound by autumn.

At the Monmouth Rowing Club, a dozen Pippa Middletons in identical leggings hauled a boat from its slumber. The boys were already on the water, being told through a megaphone to keep it up, which is surely a given when boating. I stopped at a small, plain white church that was beautiful because of – not in spite of – its modesty. An important aspect of religion must be humility, and rarely is such a quality suggested by religious buildings. The more lavish the building, it can often seem, the more impertinent its clergy.

My thought of the day was mercifully cut short by the noise of the A40, as its evergreen cargo hurried this and that to here and there: beans to Bangor, keyboards to Cardiff. I waved at a passing holiday coach and a lady waved back excitedly, honouring the unspoken and anomalous fraternity that exists between those on their holidays.

I turned on my heel and headed back to Monmouth, thinking as I did so about the various walking couples I had passed over the preceding hour: he in front with a stick, she scurrying behind; she pushing on impatiently, he dawdling to pick flowers; the couple hand-in-hand no matter the terrain. Each formation, it felt, suggested a version of loving.

At the end of Chapter Eleven, Bryson can be found dangling off a woodland precipice by his necktie, requiring some tea and a change of underpants. I, on the other hand, cannot. Instead, I can be found on my way to Oxford, safe in the knowledge that every mimic must draw the line somewhere.

12

Oxford

I went to Oxford by train, changing at Newport, which is not something I would recommend. That said, it is surely better to change at Newport than stay there. I had just 30 minutes to wander around, which was more than enough. I don't wish to be unkind, and judge a place too quickly and based on so little, but it will take a very persuasive person to tempt me back. I am quite sure that beneath the surface there is an abundance of warmth and humour and decency. But I am also quite sure that on the surface there isn't. The town seemed anxious and unwell, as if it had just been signed off work with stress. Nothing appeared to be at ease or in a state of completion, everything either going up or coming down, but mostly the latter. Outside a newsagent's, a bill for the local paper announced: 'Morris Dancer Wanted'. It was impossible to decide whether the editor felt the Morris Dancer to be the cause of all that was wrong with Newport, or its solution.

I was first in Oxford as a seventeen year old, when I attended an interview at the university. I was never a good student, preferring to spend my time playing football or socialising rather than overcoming quadratic equations. But I had a decent memory and could spend a few hours the night before an exam ingesting what I needed to know and then effectively excrete it all the next morning. Needless to say, after the exam I was as stupid as I had been two days before.

After school I went to the worst college in Hampshire, where I came out of my first year with maximum grades, albeit in far from academic subjects: psychology, sports science (which was essentially an extended table-tennis tournament), and media studies. Having got wind of my grades, a well-meaning teacher at my old school got in touch to say that such universities as Oxford were obligated to interview a quota of dipsticks from 'difficult backgrounds' and, confident I fell into such a category, suggested I put in an application. I still have a photocopy of that application, of which two-thirds were spent talking up my golf game.

Regardless, I was summoned to a three-day interview, which I enjoyed very much. I was asked by a couple of dons what my favourite book was. I didn't really have much to choose from – I had only read three or four by that time – and so gave an honest answer, *Bridget Jones's Diary*, suggesting it to be both a fine example of the epistolary form and evidence of a new perspective on the relation between identity and calorie intake. We all had a right laugh at this, and I left the interview feeling that I had made a couple of friends. When I later discussed my interview with fellow candidates, they told me categorically that the interview was not meant to be enjoyed, and that I better start considering other options. Of course I was rejected, though I did receive a kind letter explaining the decision, and some encouragement to consider the universities of Swansea and Bradford, whose canteens were known to be short of staff.

That was ten years ago, and I hadn't been back to Oxford since. Emerging from the train station into some sort of weather, the first thing I noticed was the university's new

Business School. Through the long stretches of plate glass, I watched MBA students lined up behind a parapet of laptops, contriving new ways to deregulate and tax-dodge. (What a cynic!) Between the puddles and traffic of George Street, caricatures at both ends of the social spectrum hastened here and there: a foppish student in boat shoes going decisively to a lecture; an oily mechanic encouraging his partner in confident terms to sort out a babysitter.

I too was moving decisively. I had to get to the Ashmolean Museum before it closed so I could tick it off my to-do list. The museum opened 400 years ago, and, just my luck, was due to close in an hour. As I ping-ponged around the museum's floors, I couldn't help wondering several things: whether the many portraits of this or that nobleperson were the equivalent of modern selfies, with their obvious narcissism and concern with social status; whether the many biblical paintings were the equivalent of glossy posters of modern idols such as Katy Perry or Kanye West; and whether the still lifes of fruit and pheasants and hunks of bread were the equivalent of high-res photography of toilet paper and chewing gum.

You see, once one accepts the technique and composition to be exemplary, a great majority of such paintings and *objets d'art* can prove – to my swampy mind at least – rather underwhelming. If a museum holds several thousand such objects, therefore, it stands to offer an altogether underwhelming afternoon. Of course there are those people who will – by habit or by force – profess their undying love for this sort of thing whether they like it or not ('Oh this early Rubens of out-of-date apples is simply *divine*'); and there are those who are suitably imaginative to be able to appreciate the artwork in relation to the context in which it was made ('But you have to recall, Jeremiah, that they didn't have chewing gum back then, so we have to put up with this bowl of fruit'). But to do the latter is actually rather hard, and to do the former a betrayal, to a greater or lesser degree, of snobbery and dependent thinking.

I am not saying that artworks need to be contemporary to be of interest, of course not. What I am saying is that the majority of artworks that I find valuable or moving are somehow conversant with my own experience of being alive. It is rock music and graphic novels and politically-minded comedians; it is Hopper and Lowrý and Larkin; it is *Coronation Street* and *The Wire* and *Bridget Jones's Diary*. With this in mind, perhaps it's not surprising that I found the sight of children flicking each other with orange juice in the museum's cafe, and the nicely dressed couple discussing their nicely dressed salads, and the patience shown by one waiter to another (the one having upended the tea tray of the other), immeasurably more moving and instructive than any of the Ashmolean's precious pieces. Maybe I'm just a philistine. Who cares?

In The Grapes on George Street I considered my accommodation options, which, no matter how you looked at them, weren't great. Oxford was jampacked. There was a Quidditch tournament (or similar) going on and all the hostels and cheaper hotels were full. I posted an emergency request on the couchsurfing website but knew I was unlikely to get a response that evening. Then I remembered a friend once saying that some of the university colleges let rooms to visiting dons and waifish strays, and so I set off to a call on a few of them, hoping to be mistaken for one or the other.

I tried at Nuffield and St Peter's but was told to sling my hook. At Christ Church the kindly porter spent twenty minutes trying to get me a room at the Premier Inn on Cowley Road before growing frustrated with the automated phone service and telling me much the same thing. At Merton there were no rooms available but there was a remembrance service about to start, which I was welcome to attend. Worried that I wouldn't last the whole 90 minutes, I sat at the end of a pew towards the back. Throughout the service, it was difficult to judge when one was and wasn't supposed to stand up, which made for a few embarrassing moments. As the choir made a start on 'Away in a Manger', for example, I was the only other person on my feet. Afterwards, during the drinks reception, I enjoyed eavesdropping on a ring of vicars discussing Chelsea's equaliser, which, I gathered, shouldn't have been a penalty.

Reluctant to return to the streets, I took a turn about the college, hoping to bump into one of the dons that interviewed me ten years before and maybe secure some digs. (What are pals for, huh?) In a basement launderette, I overheard in relation to a pair of socks a discussion of post-Kantian aesthetics, which I found rather indulgent. (I mean to say, do undergraduates really need to be washing their socks?) Then I happened upon the college's dining room, where a hundred or so students were enjoying a roast dinner. Not really knowing what to do with myself, I soon had the attention of the crowd, who seemed slightly alarmed to see me but hesitant to alert security in case I was that evening's guest speaker. I was eventually escorted off

96   OXFORD

the premises by a Latvian porter, who found me queuing for a bowl of crumble.

I don't know why exactly, but all the while I was going about town that evening I felt a dull, general sadness. I remember on several occasions having tears in my eyes – in The Grapes, during the remembrance service, as I was pulled away from my crumble. Perhaps because I had memories of failing here, everything around me felt like a reminder of not being good enough. To escape these feelings, I steered clear of the colleges for an hour or so, and walked instead around Oxford's regrettable ring road, taking solace in the meaningless loop of traffic which reminded me of nothing.

Sat at a bus stop with a kebab, I got a call from a friend who had seen my accommodation enquiry on Facebook. My friend explained that his sister lived in Oxford and that she would come and collect me when she was finished eating at a Lebanese restaurant, which is exactly what she did, thanks be to the Lord (and my friend and his sister and anyone else implicated in my good fortune). As we walked down High Street and across Magdalen Bridge towards the Cowley Road, my saviour probed me in the flippant fashion particular to Oxbridge students – What do you do? Why do you do *that*? What do you mean you don't ski? – but by the time we reached her place she had begun to soften, perhaps sensing that it was unlikely I'd ever be competing with her for a promotion. I remain in her debt.

For Bryson, Oxford has a special place on his list of things that Brits love that he doesn't, a list that includes Sooty, Marmite,

Bill and Ben the flowerpot men, George Formby and *Dixon of Dock Green*. It would seem to me, given the above, that it would be a very good thing for Bryson if Britain returned to the punitive strategies of the Middle Ages and started chopping people's hands off for the slightest misdemeanours. For without hands Bryson's sick-bucket-list would all but disappear. They'd certainly be no Sooty, it would be tough to spread Marmite, Bill and Ben would remain prostrate in their pots, Formby would be forced to play the banjo with his arm-ends and soon give up, and Dixon of Dock Green would find it hard to cuff anyone. Just a thought.

More to the point though is *why* Bryson includes Oxford in such a disreputable group. Its donnishness is one reason. What, Bill begs, 'now that Britain no longer needs colonial administrators who can quip in Latin', is all this intellectual toil *for*? Can Britain really afford to be so intellectually minded at a time when it's reliant on Samsung to provide jobs? What's going to put food on the nation's table in about 2010?

Well, if the current higher education landscape is anything to go by, it certainly isn't the humanities that are being trusted to put food on the table. Such departments as philosophy, literature and foreign languages are shrinking or closing every day, as the academic focus – and with it the funding – is shifted significantly onto subjects like engineering and the sciences.

This might be all very well, and in keeping with the dominant capitalist ideology, which makes a fetish of economic growth, but it would surely be wise to keep an eye on the effects, both social and economic, of such a bias. There's a nice indelicate satirical dystopian short story to be written, I feel, about a dinner party in the future whose guests spend the evening gorging on cutting-edge food and drink but don't talk because they've forgotten how to. At the end of the meal, the dinner table collapses under the weight of the food on top of it, and everyone gets trapped beneath it and dies, apart from the descendant of a philosopher-poet, who happened to be in the loo at the time. The moral of the story? Not all wealth can be counted. So beware false prophets.

Such reflections had given me an appetite, so upon Bryson's recommendation I headed to Browns in north Oxford. It's still a convivial and classy joint, I'm pleased to report, and you can still order a bacon-cheeseburger and a Caesar salad, and so I did. At a nearby table, a set of grandparents were treating their granddaughter and two of her friends to lunch. From what I could gather, the granddaughter and her friends had started their degrees at the university just a few weeks earlier. When they came to order, the young students all went for the salad niçoise. The grandparents glanced at each other uncertainly (as if to say, 'Wtf?') before silently agreeing that this must be the only respectable thing on the menu and ordering likewise. I am genuinely not sure if anything like this will ever happen again, in Browns or elsewhere. I mean, five tuna salads?

For the rest of the meal, the grandparents leant forwards over their salads deferentially, in thrall to the stories of Oxford life. As if to counter the enthusiasm of the grandparents, and so doing accentuate it, as the students told their stories they adopted more and more irreverent postures, leaning back in their chairs, crossing their arms, putting their feet up on nearby tables (my table!). If the generosity of the grandparents had stretched to dessert, the younger trio might well have lit cigars and used grandmother's handbag as an ashtray.

I exaggerate of course, but as the meal went on there really was a discernible change in the tone and manners of the students, as if with each minute and anecdote that passed they began to believe that, yes, we *do* deserve deference, you two are *right* to be in thrall, I *am* special. If this was the effect of three weeks, what of three years at Oxford? To be fair to them though, it was the students, and not the grandparents, that insisted on leaving a tip.

After my lunch, I went to a bookshop on nearby Walton Street, where I was told by the proprietor that I should be retracing J.B. Priestley not Bryson. If I wanted to see how a place had changed, he went on, you start further back, and you don't pick an author (brilliant though he is) who is known to prioritise comic digressions over careful description. 'Priestley travelled in 1933, and he wrote about the people and their work, about local government and poverty and manufacturing. What are you going to write about? Bacon-cheeseburgers?' I gave this some thought – or affected to at least. 'If you ask me,' the bookseller resumed, 'you should have waited until 2033 and then done the centenary of Priestley.'

I'm not an impatient person, but twenty years does seem a long time to wait before making a start on something. When I pointed this out, the proprietor just smiled and gave a friendly nod in the direction of the door.

I took the hint and went to the Sheldonian Theatre, Wren's debut in 1669. It is at the Sheldonian that Oxford's students graduate, so I had a bit of fun by getting up on the stage and awarding myself an honorary degree for failing to distinguish myself in any field. Up in the cupola of the theatre, I looked down on Oxford. I saw Broad Street laden with diagonally parked cars; labourers in orange tending to the roof of a library they'll never enter; the Bridge of Sighs, upon which undergrads whimper after making a dog's dinner of their finals; gables and statues and umbrellas and bicycles; a string of tourists in anoraks; a college flag trying to flutter; and, last but not least, just visible in the distance, a student at her desk with a cup of something hot, bent over this or that masterpiece, a salad niçoise at hand, a pencil behind an ear, another Barbara Castle or Iris Murdoch or Nigella Lawson in the making.

Watching the young woman at her desk, it was impossible to be cynical. As much as I willed there to be so, there was no trace of arrogance or entitlement in her face, only a look of quiet determination and absorption. I tend to get a bit bristly and socialist when I'm in a place like Oxford, so it's good to have moments like this one now, when you see clearly that the objects of one's discontent – the students washing their socks, ordering salad, asking 'What do you mean you don't ski?' – are for the most part just good people doing good things in a good place. If I have issues, they are with the system and not the personnel. It's just hard to poke a system in the eye, I guess. I wished the anonymous scholar well – very well – and descended once more unto the street.

13

Cotswolds

The car rental company wanted to see the paper copy of my licence before handing over the keys, which struck me as somewhat archaic, akin to demanding an umbilical cord as a form of identification. I didn't have the paper copy, I hadn't seen it for years, not since I lent it to a cousin so they could get into the only club in Portsmouth that cared how old anyone was, and so I had to pay a £25 surcharge so the rental company could call someone up to check I was legit. When I was eventually issued the car, I had, contra Bryson, absolutely no trouble ascertaining what the various stalks and switches were for. If Bryson is to be believed, he could barely identify the steering wheel. Should we really be allowing such an easily dumbfounded fellow to write popular science books?

I drove to Woodstock, which as in '94 sits ten miles north of Oxford. I parked the car and took a look at the town. More than elsewhere, there was a strong sense that things hadn't changed much, and were unlikely to do so anytime soon. I put this to three older women loitering in a bookshop.

'The only thing that changes is the mood of the duke,' said one of them.

'Is this your husband?' I asked. They all gasped.

'The Duke of *Marlborough*. He lives at the palace. And for

your information he goes for continental women. The Duchess is Spanish. Or Cuban. One of the two.'[2]

I went to Blenheim Palace, knowing a few things about the place. I knew that it was awarded to the first Duke of Marlborough – one John Churchill – about three centuries ago to honour his military successes. I knew that the sum awarded by parliament to construct the property was much smaller than the ambitions of the architect, who Churchill had commissioned in a moment of drunken whimsy at a London playhouse. The architect – John Vanbrugh – was actually a gardener or something, but had been so persuasive during the interval of *Titus Andronicus* that Churchill was all for it.

Unsurprisingly, the money ran out with only the kitchen and the miniature railway completed, leaving Churchill to borrow and beg to get the thing finished, which it eventually was, about 30 years after the first brick was laid. Despite being heavily indebted by this point, Churchill made sure to crown his estate with a giant memorial to himself. Rumour has it that the duke would spend Tuesday mornings climbing the 60-foot column to make sure his likeness wasn't showing signs of age.

It was at the base of this column that I now stood, having entered the palace's grounds via a green door opposite The Black Prince pub. I had initially tried to enter through the official portal, but was scared off by the asking price. The young man guarding the official portal, sensing my discomfiture, had the grace to reveal that I could access the grounds for free via

---

[2] She's Iranian.

a public right of way, so long as I didn't, at any point, turn left and venture toward the palace itself.

I turned left and ventured toward the palace itself, passing a dozen pheasants sitting on the fence regarding a sycamore tree. (I don't mean to say that the pheasants were *unsure* about the tree, but that they were, quite literally, sitting on a fence regarding it.) All was caught in mist – the lake and brook and the wet black trees with their conflicting wigs of bright dying leaves.

Skulking in the distance was the buttery spread of the palace. If ever a building could be accused of arrogance it was this one. Though I suppose we should be grateful that it's here at all, for it was almost ruined about a hundred years ago. After the seventh duke had spent what was left of the family cash on fast cars, the eighth was forced to flog all the expensive paintings to keep the bulldozers at bay, and the ninth, bless him, to marry a rich American girl just to keep the wolf from the door. The American girl's parents, in thrall to all things British and aristocratic, desperately wanted a duchess of a daughter, and so paid the ninth duke the equivalent of $65 million to take their dearest darling daughter under his wing. Leaving the church after their wedding, the duke is known to have turned to his young wife and said: 'Now let's get one thing straight: I'm in love with another woman and despise all things not British.' Charming.

It is perhaps unsurprising, given the ninth duke's outspoken patriotism, to learn that Winston Churchill, poster boy of British statesmen, was a nephew. Winston took regular minibreaks at the palace, where he would contrive foreign policy riding the miniature steam train. He must have fallen off once, because he's buried just around the corner at Bladon, where I went now. In the churchyard dark, I tried hard to maintain a respectful frame of mind as I stood over Churchill's plot; but I couldn't help thinking of all the surrounding graves, as real and definitive as Churchill's, and yet so less regarded, so less cared about on a national level. Returning to the car through rush-hour drizzle, it occurred to me that only when all are treated equally in death, no matter rank or role or race, will the world seem to me a calmer, more honourable place. Inside the car, steady rain drumming on the roof, I sat pensively for a few minutes, trying to work out how to activate the windscreen wipers.

I stayed the night at the Frogmill Inn, which is somewhere in the Cotswolds. I can be no more precise because I arrived there during a heavy fog, which concealed road signs and anything else that might have given a clue where I was. In the dining room the next morning, my breakfast was greatly improved by eavesdropping on a middle-aged couple at the next table. One by one they complimented the breakfast items. He would propose the mushroom to be of a good size; she would confirm that it was. She would propose the yolk to be nice and yellow; he would confirm that it was. And so it went on until all items had been duly considered. I don't mean to mock the couple, or to suggest that their careful deconstruction of breakfast hinted at a failed marriage. Quite the opposite. Their conversation – if it can be called such – was tender and heartfelt and actually rather touching. What tickled me most though was when I learned that they had been staying at the Frogmill for nearly a week. Did they do this each morning? I was tempted to stay another night just to find out.

The day was bright. As I slowly drove nowhere in particular, my appreciation for the countryside roundabout was greater for having arrived in the dark and fog. You could say that I woke up to the Cotswolds rather than entered them. My mood was also buoyed by the car, and the licence it afforded to zip here and there as I wished. At one point I was prevented turning left because the road was being repaired. I interpreted the diversion not as a setback but as an opportunity to see another way, which proved delicious, running as it did along the ridge of an escarpment, flanking trees creating a tunnel of branches, through which came flashes of sun and glimpses of yonder valleys. It was all very pleasing. At one point, as I bore down on Upper Slaughter and 'Teenage Kicks' by The Undertones came on the radio, it was all I could do not to stick my head through the sunroof and whoop.

Walking into Upper Slaughter, having parked just outside, I read on a community notice board that the main item of discussion at the forthcoming AGM would be 'kitchen extensions'. Further along, I passed a gardener tidying a hedgerow. All of his features were bulbous and manic, his eyes and sideburns in particular. I asked if much had changed in the area since he last trimmed his sideburns.

'Japanese,' he said.

Unsure if this was a question or not, I sort of frowned and cocked my head at the same time.

'Japanese *tourists*,' he continued furtively, as if fearful of being overheard. 'They love it. And they love a picture. If they was 'ere now they'd want one of us.'

I expressed surprise at this.

'Problem is the local vicar's an epileptic.'

I said that I was sorry to hear it.

'Yeah but the thing is he didn't 'ave it before they all started taking pictures of everything, did he?'

Sensing he was getting a bit worked up, I changed the subject. 'What about immigration?'

'Weekenders!' It sounded like a new soap opera. 'Folk from London buying 'ouses for the weekends.'

'And is this problem across the—'

'And of course the 'ouse prices go up! My son had to move to Newport of all places. His kids 'ave only been down 'ere once. I've swapped my family for a load of photographers.' I looked down, kicked the grass, exhaled sympathetically. 'If you've any sense at all you'll turn round and go 'ome,' he said.

I didn't know what to do. This last was said so plaintively, so sorrowfully, that it wasn't easy to brush off as rhetoric. If I heeded this man and turned around I would feel meek and foolish. If I ignored him and continued down to the village, I would, in effect, be admitting to having no sense at all. In the end, I waited for him to resume trimming the hedgerow before pressing on behind his back.

Cut from the golden limestone that lends the Cotswolds its famous glow, Upper Slaughter is a very picturesque village indeed, and I encourage you to go there at once. It has a sweet river, on which a dozen well-to-do ducks can be seen swimming back and forth discussing the matters of the day. It has a nice bric-a-brac shop called the Old Mill, a nice pub, and a cute little hotel. It has a small becoming church and some green space for the only child in the village to make use of. Despite its charm, however, I resisted the temptation to take a photo, lest the vicar got wind of it.

I returned to the car and moved on to Broadway, where I was told that my shoes wouldn't cope. I wanted to visit Broadway Tower – a hilltop folly awarded to the Earl of Coventry many moons ago – and would have to pass a boggy meadow to do so. Not wanting to ruin my only shoes, I took a different route, which incorporated a winding dual carriageway and a couple of barbed wire fences. When I reached the folly, torn and breathless, the gentleman responsible for its retail operation asked if, for a fiver, I wanted to climb the tower. I pointed out that I was already 1,080 metres above sea level, the highest point in the Cotswolds, and asked what good another twenty would do me. He said it would help keep him in a job.

The view from the tower was eminently better than the one twenty metres below. The broad Vale of Evesham, with its 'gently undulating trapezoids of farmland', was a pleasure to behold. Just about audible was the hum of the A40, the very hum that stalked me as I walked the River Wye in Monmouth. The sound of traffic drew my mind to the less bucolic features of the landscape – the power stations, housing estates and warehouses noted by Bryson – each steadily claiming a greater share of the canvas.

Bryson warns that we are half a generation away from destroying our countryside. I'm not by instinct a conservationist, and won't pretend to be, but stood where I was, my thoughts led by Bryson's harsh prophesy, I couldn't help but feel a little ashamed that I give such things so little thought. If you multiply my attitude by 8.5 billion, then you have a much-endangered planet, or, at the very least, one that is set to grow uglier and more troublesome with age. J.B. Priestley, when he stood on this spot 80 years ago, said that 'we ought to take the whole of that countryside and lay it on our consciences', which is almost certainly true, but almost certainly easier said than done.

I went next to Evesham because I was told it's unpleasant. The general prettiness of Broadway and Upper Slaughter had become a little saccharine, and I wanted a corrective to it, so I'd asked the man guarding the folly if there was somewhere horrible in the Cotswolds and he'd volunteered Evesham, about ten miles north.

I parked on the edge of town and took a slow, curious walk in. According to a sandwich board outside a pub, a band called Stiff Upper Lip was set to play that night, followed by Irony a few nights later. This information actually stopped me in my tracks. Was it not peculiar that a man travelling Britain, sensitive to that nation's stereotypical features, keen, even, to testify against them, happened to walk past a pub in the Cotswolds whose forthcoming entertainment was a punk band called Stiff Upper Lip and a jazz trio called Irony? It is the sort of coincidence a novelist might use to give a quirky sense of place or to serve as a portent. I wonder who's due to play next month. I wouldn't be surprised if it was a band called Milky Tea and a solo artist called Inflexible Class System.

Further along, the main bridge into town was shut off to all traffic. Given the volume of immigration that Evesham has experienced over the last few years (which is why, I soon realised, I had been sent here), it wouldn't surprise me if the bridge were being demolished to curb the influx.

It is the fertility of the surrounding land, and the consequent agriculture, that has made Evesham popular with EU immigrants, and Poles in particular. When Poland joined the EU in 2004 its citizens were afforded the right to work and live in Britain. Many exercised their right, about 1.2 million in fact, ten times more than the British government anticipated, which is perhaps one of the reasons why that government was quick to assure us that the Poles were here to do the jobs that no one else wanted, which is a better thing to say than there's been a complete balls-up.

It wasn't until the recent global recession (circa 2007–10) that mainstream opinion began to grow critical of immigration levels. In all ranks of life, Brits could be seen and heard slowly raising their eyebrows at the status quo (if that's even possible). And I can understand why they might have done, for at the same time that the British people were being told to brace themselves for comprehensive cuts to public spending on account of the country's poor finances, they were also being told to tolerate further immigration. It may well be the case that immigrants tend to boost economies rather than drain them, but nevertheless, one doesn't have to be a racist or xenophobe to look at that somewhat paradoxical scenario – less money, more people – to feel a measure of unease or confusion.

I asked the bookkeeper at William Hill if the Poles had been made to feel welcome in Evesham. She answered by pointing out that the Romans weren't popular when they turned up either. I asked her to elaborate and she said that no matter the circumstances, immigrant ideas, habits and languages will always be liable to unsettle those that are unfamiliar with them, particularly if said immigrants make no effort to 'adapt to the way we do things here'. I suggested that 'the way we do things here' was perhaps too vague a code of conduct to be useful. She gave an exaggerated shrug, before admitting that she doesn't actually care too much if they adapt or not, so long as they don't do any harm.

Returning to the car, I speculated that if the people of the UK do have a chronic problem regarding groups that refuse to adapt or make concessions in the interests of social harmony and justice etc, then those groups are the very wealthy and the very important, who, by and large, will do all they can (and they can do a lot) to rig the system and steer mass opinion to their advantage. I have far more in common, I thought, once more trying to start the wipers, with a Polish immigrant who can't yet speak English than I do with most of those that purport to represent me in the House of Commons, or those that have extreme wealth or influence, who ought to be subjected to far more suspicion than Polish immigrants picking asparagus. And with that I put the radio on and drove away.

14

Milton Keynes–Cambridge–Newmarket

I drove without issue to Oxford, whence I took a train to London and then another to Milton Keynes, a town I was not in a hurry to see, having been told that it was like a German airport without the sense of anticipation. My friend Anthony was also not in a hurry to see Milton Keynes and so came with me. We spent most of the train journey from London Euston trying to find a kid picking his nose (Bill had sat opposite such a child) but found only adults behaving thus.

Bryson didn't do a great deal in Milton Keynes, partly because he only intended to stop for lunch en route to Cambridge, and partly because he couldn't find anything *to* do. In fact, most of his time here seems to have been spent lost in one of the town's several million underpasses, desperately hoping to find his way back to the shopping centre where he could get a cup of coffee at a grubby McDonald's.

Milton Keynes is rational to an insane degree. Despite its 'rational' design, however, it is oddly disorientating. But it is not disorientating in the nice way that Venice or Strasbourg are, where getting lost is somehow part of the charm. Moreover, cities like Venice and Strasbourg have pleasing landmarks and features from which one can recover their bearings: a cutesy gelato parlour, say, or a statue of Raymond Blanc. In contrast, because of Milton Keynes' age – it was built in the late 60s to alleviate crowding in London – and because of the rational principles that underpinned its design, when you get lost here it's hard to intuitively get back on track. One car park can only look so much different from another, and the same is true of the horizontal and vertical grid roads that form the town's chassis. The many office buildings are also eerily similar: rectangular, reflective and almost invariably TO LET.

Another reason the town is hard to navigate is because there's no one to ask for directions. Or so it can seem. The lack of human traffic is partly because the town's planners had in mind a town on a city-scale; a settlement with the population and facilities of a town but the size and infrastructure of a city. Milton Keynes has half the population of Portsmouth but double the space, making it very easy to wander around the place for two hours – taking in the vast shopping mall, the vast Campbell Park, the vast array of entertainments (ski slope, casino, concrete cows) – and not see another person. Even the 125 miles of scenic walk- and cycle-ways go mostly unused. Why? Because each of the town's 100 'grid squares' (or microcommunities) is self-sufficient, which means that no one needs to walk between them. Thus, with one aspect of their design (the self-sufficient grid-squares) the town planners negated the need for another (the 125 miles of pedestrian ways). How rational is that?

But this lack of conviviality, of hustle and bustle, wouldn't disappoint the man whose ideas inspired and guided Milton Keynes' development. Melvin Webber was a German-American architect and urban theorist in thrall to modernist and rationalist principles. According to Webber (and his mentor Ludwig Mies), buildings – and by extension towns and cities – should be no more than 'skin and bones', shorn of anything superfluous like, I don't know, a heart. Further, Webber considered traditional town planning models to be outmoded because of new communication and travel abilities, holding that in the modern age people socialise and trade in more virtual, disembodied ways, and that a new town ought to facilitate and reflect such changes.

If the nature of a town's layout and buildings says something about the values and attitude of its epoch, what does Milton Keynes say about us (or, if not us, then the dominant ideology that steers us)? That we are self-centred rather than communal? That we are rigid rather than flexible? That we are heartless? One thing a town like Milton Keynes certainly intimates is that our instincts and predispositions are increasingly American. The town's landmark building is a central glass tower called Manhattan House, and its road signs don't direct traffic towards a centre but to its 'SHOPPING'. More than anywhere else in the UK, Milton Keynes *feels* ideological; a manifestation of a worldview. Even the sandwich shop on Midsummer Boulevard somehow echoes the town's founding principles. Behind the counter an assembly line of employees awaited my order. One of them fetched my bread; another inserted the filling; another salad and sauce; another seasoned, bagged and wondered if I wanted a cookie or a hot drink; and a final took the cash. The process was certainly effective – I was out of there within a minute – but the atomised transaction made it impossible to connect, however briefly or trivially, with any of the human constituents, making for a more efficient but less nourishing experience. It was Milton Keynes writ small.

As it happened, the reason Anthony and I chose to call it a day and return to London hadn't to do with any half-baked theoretical objections ('Ben. I've had enough. This roundabout is just too neo-liberal'), but because of Anthony's lack of wheelchair battery. I was a little put-out.

'Was it not charged last night, Anthony?'

'That's your responsibility.'

'Since when?'

'Since this morning.'

And so we made our way back to the train station and back to London, where Anthony headed home and I took a train to Cambridge.

On the equivalent train journey to Cambridge twenty years before, Bryson passed much of the time studying his map and drooling over British place names, a practice he considers 'one of the deep and abiding pleasures of life in Britain'. For Bryson, the very fact that things have names – perhaps the most basic principle of semiotics – is sufficient to keep him pumped for hours at a time. He confesses to finding 'endless satisfaction' drinking in a pub called The Lamb and Flag rather than Joe's Bar. You have to wonder just how far this peculiar sensitivity to what things are called extends. I mean, would Bryson divorce his wife Cynthia if it transpired, Oscar Wilde-style, that her real name was Ernest?

And proper nouns aren't Bill's only unlikely pastime. For such a bright man, he has some very down-to-earth predilections. Based on what I've learnt from *Notes from a Small Island*, Bryson's perfect day would involve a morning at the Tit and Barrel watching pigeons, an afternoon at a Chinese buffet with a good map for company, and then an evening in the bath listening to the shipping forecast. If he wanted to push the boat out, after his bath he'd draft a letter to *The Times* about a disrespected hedgerow. Can this guy actually be married?

Cambridge train station is at the end of Hills Street, about a mile from the town centre (yes, it has a centre). About halfway along Hills Street is the University Arms Hotel, where Bill shacked-up for the night. I sought a room there but they were full. At a loss, I poked about in Christ's Pieces (pleasantly arranged) and a few shopping streets (Green Street, Rose Crescent), before chancing upon Clare College, one of the 40 or so colleges that make up the University of Cambridge, where I asked for a room. The porter told me matter-of-factly that there were none available. I informed him, with careful ambiguity, that I was ex-Cambridge (I had, after all, been to the city before). His attitude to my predicament shifted immediately, and within minutes I was boiling the kettle in room P3 and trying on the various academic costumes that I found in the cupboard.

I took a stroll around the college to get a feel for the place. Like Oxford's, Cambridge's colleges have an unmistakable air of pre-eminence, and with good reason. For 500 years after their establishment in the 13th century the two universities (collectively known as Oxbridge) successfully petitioned the Crown to prevent the establishment of any other higher learning institutions. In effect, for half a millennium Oxbridge had a unique monopoly on higher education, and was thus able to deny such an education to all but a small elite, within whose hands knowledge (and thus power) would remain, to the benefit of a few, and the detriment of pretty much everyone else. Given the above, it is little wonder that Cambridge alone has issued 38 heads of state, nine monarchs and Stephen Fry.

The monopoly didn't last of course. Over the past century scores and scores of universities have opened their doors to school leavers hoping to continue their educations. In theory, then, more people are now acquiring the knowledge and skill sets to compete for the country's top jobs. Yet when we consider that the large majority of today's governing ministers and CEOs and VIPs studied at Oxbridge, it's easy to suspect that nothing much has changed, that Oxbridge remains the entrance point to the corridors of power. As things stand, Oxbridge serves as a peculiar dishwasher on a national level. It takes the nation's most expensive crockery and then puts it through a comprehensive cycle until it's just that little bit more sparkly. Then some lackey comes along and unthinkingly loads all the shining crockery into cupboards and draws marked The Establishment. Meanwhile, those dishes that got chipped or stained during dinner are either discarded entirely or scrubbed by hand with the cheapest detergent, before being stored in low cupboards marked This Will Have to Do. But here's the thing: all the crockery is made of the same stuff; it just gets treated differently.[3]

---

[3] Note to self. Never again embark upon an extended metaphor involving a dishwasher.

I left the college and, on a whim, entered the Corpus Christi Playhouse, where I saw a First World War drama that was so true to life that it was practically insufferable. Afterwards I repaired to a pub called the Bath House, where I drank several consoling pints of Indian Pale Ale and witnessed the second half of another England–Germany fixture, this one settled with a header that beat the goalkeeper at his near post. Following Bryson's lead, I then sought out a 'mediocre' curry house and an 'empty pub for a lonely pint'. It was hard to find a curry house that would admit to being mediocre, much easier to find a pub that was empty. It was six quid a pint at The Fountain which is probably why it had no custom. I queried the price.

'It's a craft beer. Small batches.'

'I don't care if it was crafted in Machu Picchu by the Dalai Lama, that's ridiculous.'

And then Gary Gunn entered, looking like a toothless De Niro, and immediately got wound up because the pub didn't serve his preferred cider. I didn't want Gunn to notice the young lady to his right, so I asked him what part of London he was from, and got this in reply:

'Whatever bit I fucking well like. I'm the craziest bastard you'll ever meet. Ex-SAS. You know Maggie? 1982. She phoned me up. What do you want? I said. Gary, go and have a look would you. Falklands. So I went over by submarine. Course I did. It was like Clapham bloody Common. There was this bloke living in a shed. I knocked on his door with my gun. Course I did. He said come in for tea.'

'That's nice.'

'But I only drink Assam.'

'Assam?'

'Assam. But he didn't have it. So I shot him.'

'Bit of an overreaction.'

'Don't judge me. Don't fucking judge me. Oi, barman, get this bloke a drink.'

I was tempted to get another pint of the Machu Picchu stuff. 'Gary, I can't. I've got to go.'

'No you haven't. No you fucking haven't. Get this bloke a fucking drink.'

'No, really, I've got a date.'

'Ah, fair enough. Off you go then.'

Then he gave me directions (precise and accurate, as it happens) to the curry house I had just been to, shook my hand, bade me farewell. A part of me was reluctant to leave. Not because I was enjoying Mr Gunn's company – I felt constantly one slip away from a smack in the mouth – but because I could sense that the others in the pub would have even less time for him than I had, which would only wind him up further.

I retraced my steps back to Clare College and had a pint in the college bar. The bar was full of women. This pleased me, for such a sight would have been unthinkable only a few decades ago. To be fair, Cambridge (Oxford also) has come a long way and now admits as many women as men to its colleges, but the grain against which such measures are counteracting is a deep and stubborn one, and despite such consoling statistics as a 50:50 split at Oxbridge, there remains a damaging inequality (actual and attitudinal) both in and out of the workplace. This is perhaps unsurprising when it is borne in mind that the first all-male college at Cambridge to admit women did so only

40 years ago, a mere sniff when compared to the 800 years of all-male education that came before it. You might say that the lads got one hell of a head start. In this light, it is probably not off the mark to say that proper fairness in this country regarding working opportunities remains in its infancy. To see its advance into adulthood – when no one will blink to see a boardroom dominated by women, or, on the other hand, to see men raising children – will require a great deal more agitation, by women and men. I for one will be more than willing to stay at home while my partner goes out to work. And what's more, I'd be willing to do this long before we even thought of having children.

The next morning, after some eggs Florentine and a ristretto, I went to Cambridge's other university – Anglia Ruskin. I had arranged to meet with a Brazilian exchange student to discuss her thoughts on Cambridge. As I waited outside the library, perhaps a hundred students shuffled past. Not one of them was white. They weren't international students. They were British. Sure, Cambridge University has non-white students, but they're mostly internationals from wealthy backgrounds. Ruskin, which is at the other end of the university spectrum to Cambridge, is full of Britain's ethnic and racial minorities. For fear of banging a drum, I will say only that I had a strong urge to unilaterally clear a portion of Clare College and rehouse a batch of Ruskin students there, and so doing sow the seeds for a new batch of ministers and monarchs and national treasures.

The Brazilian, whose lecture had overrun, eventually collected me and took me to her student dormitory, where we ate 'Fish-style Fingers' and drank lunchtime whisky. We spoke about Rio and corruption and the Brazilian government's attempts, in the run up to the Olympics in 2016, to clear certain slums – ones that tourists might chance upon after a beach volleyball match – of drug dealers et al., which, once cleared, tend to have their power vacuums readily filled with one militia or another (see Iraq, Syria, Libya, Afghanistan …). I forgot to ask about Cambridge.

I was introduced to a young man called Alvaro who produces portraits of famous literary figures with a typewriter, and together the three of us rode bicycles across Parker's Piece and Midsummer Common and through the Grafton Shopping Centre and along Mill Road, arriving, coincidentally, back at The Fountain. I asked the barman how long Gary Gunn had stuck around the night before and he said long enough to start threatening to kill someone and upending tables. I asked what became of him. 'He was carried away by six policemen.' Perhaps I should have accepted his offer of a pint.

I had to get a move on. I had to reach Reach. It is at Reach that one can pick up the western end of the Devil's Dyke, an earthen embankment that runs in a straight line for seven miles to Ditton Green. Bryson described the experience of walking along it as 'a trifle dull', but I was determined to undertake it nonetheless. Getting to the dyke proved a pain in the neck, mind you. Instead of taking the direct bus from Cambridge as normal people might have done, I plotted a shortcut that first involved taking a train to Waterbeach, whence I could cannily pick up a footpath which would take me to a point a couple of miles along the dyke, allowing me to reach its terminus before sunset.

I never found the footpath because a lady in the queue at the Waterbeach post office wouldn't let me go after it. Instead, she insisted that it would be a better idea if she drove me to Burwell, where I could access the dyke easily and save some time. And she was right. It would have been a good idea for her to drive me to Burwell, where I could access the dyke easily and save some time, only she didn't do that, she drove me to Stow-cum-Quy, which is about seven miles from anywhere. Of course she *thought* she had dropped me in Burwell, but in these situations it isn't the thought that counts. So if you happen upon a friendly grandmother of three called Janice who is oftentimes heading to Newmarket to collect her youngest descendants, remember me to her would you, in whatever terms you prefer.

After being deposited, I walked a few hundred metres along a busy road until I came to a pub, where I sought further directions, sensing that something was amiss. It was here that I learnt about Janice's terrific cock-up. A very old man, who was just finishing a prawn cocktail, overheard my conversation with the barmaid and informed me that he had to be in Exney for a dental appointment by half past one. I wanted to ask how his having a dental appointment in Exney at half past one got me any closer to where I needed to be, but chose not to, because he was a dear old boy, and so I smiled instead and said I'd give the bus a go, which met a chorus of ooohhs and good-luck-with-thats.

Their scepticism proved well-founded when the number ten bus ignored my elaborate flagging and drove straight past me, its driver evidently satisfied that half-a-dozen passengers was more than enough. It was now approaching 2 and I had, I reckoned, at least four hours of walking ahead of me. I considered throwing in the towel and taking a bus back to Cambridge, but was prevented from doing so by the Clarkes, who had noticed my disquiet and offered to run me somewhere in their car.

As we whizzed along in his Honda convertible, I learnt that Mr Clarke was a banker in Peterborough between 1984 and 1988; that he and his wife are proactively right-wing; and that the Poles in Peterborough had dramatically – dramatically! – affected the character of the town. I told Mr Clarke – upon exiting his vehicle – that although Bryson hadn't stopped in Peterborough I would visit the town and give some thought to the Polish Dramatic Society rumoured to be running riot there. He gave a satisfied nod, and then zipped off into the future.[4]

---

[4] Peterborough was a bit disappointing to be frank. Contrary to what Mr Clarke had promised, there were no Poles causing havoc in the street, or drinking theatrically in the park, or overrunning public services. That's not to say there aren't Poles in Peterborough, for there surely are. Conservative estimates (no pun intended) suggest that Poles make up 10 per cent of the local population. Perhaps I just caught Peterborough on a bad day. Perhaps all the Poles were indoors rehearsing a Gilbert and Sullivan piece. Who knows? Returning to Peterborough station after my lap of town, I spotted a poster in the window of a cafe which pictorially suggested that it was quite possible for the entire contents of a full English breakfast ('2 egg, 2 bacon, 2 sausage, black pudding, mushrooms, beans,

I found the dyke and quickly got on with my walking, pass-ing windmills and fields and red berries on otherwise bare winter bushes. I crossed a slice of motorway and entered the grounds of Newmarket Racecourse, where I did unseen fur-longs while eating a sandwich. At the end of the racecourse the dyke continues for another couple of miles before it runs into inconsequential fields near the village of Ditton Green. I derived from Bryson's account that there wasn't much going on in Ditton Green and so I declined the final stretch of the dyke and hung a left toward Newmarket, where I thought I might spend a profitable hour wandering before taking a train back to Cambridge.

At the edge of town I asked a dog walker where I might get a half-decent cup of coffee. He answered by drawing a map in the dewy grass with a tennis ball launcher. He did this with such seriousness that he might have been plotting a piece of geopolitical subterfuge. For about ten minutes he scored fault lines and clandestine alleys into the damp green canvas, giv-ing his dog the opportunity, which it duly seized, to disappear unnoticed. It was only when I brought his dog's disappearance to the man's attention that he withdrew his launcher from the grass and strode off anxiously without so much as a goodbye.

When I got to the centre of town, I was struck by the num-ber of betting shops. I went into one and put £5 each-way on Archie Rice at 16/1. Unbidden, the bookmaker mentioned

tomatoes, fried bread, tea or coffee') to be sandwiched into an eight-inch bread-roll. Now call me pitiless, but if the cafe proprietors of Peterborough keep promising such things, they've only themselves to blame if the town continues to attract new residents.

a man who was stabbed seven times in the housing estate across the road. (Personally, if I got stabbed once somewhere, I wouldn't make a habit of going back.) As we talked through bulletproof glass, a punter approached and called the book-maker several names under the sun, on account of a horse not finishing where it was supposed to in the 4.30 at Kempton Park. I understood why the guy was upset (it didn't look like he had much to lose) but suggested in any case that it was hardly Raquel's fault if Sophie's Choice didn't take to the soft conditions.

Continuing my tour, I entered the Job Centre on Wellington Street and had a go on one of the job search machines, which matched my credentials with a vacancy on a farm in Ipswich. Not exactly a beckoning opportunity. Also not exactly beck-oning was the small green at the end of the high street. The green holds a significant war memorial, which has unfortu-nately been made inaccessible by three lanes of peevish traffic. The local council, I conjectured, will soon be obliged to erect another memorial to honour those that perished trying to get to this one.

Far more beckoning was a busy delicatessen off the high street, where I asked an employee why the sausages in Newmarket are world-famous. He handed me a cooked one over the counter and whispered 'just eat that and don't make a fuss'. While eating the sausage and not making a fuss, it occurred to me that on a pleasure-per-minute basis I was hav-ing one of the best hours of my life. I considered getting a room and staying in Newmarket for a month. I could back Archie Rice and discuss social issues with Raquel. I could get in touch with the council about how dangerous the war memorial is. I could find the guy that keeps getting stabbed and tell him to do himself a favour and walk a different route to work. I could apply for the job in Ipswich. I could teach the man with the tennis-ball launcher how to end a conversation politely. But of course I couldn't stay. I had to keep moving. I had to get back in the saddle. I had to go to Retford.

15

Retford–Worksop

Our lives are shaped and coloured by the will to pleasure. To a greater or lesser extent, we are compelled to seek out those things that we have come to understand as being good and beneficial and pleasing – things like spaghetti bolognaise, Kate Bush and Norwich. Knowingly or not, the will to pleasure also compels us to *avoid* those things that we have come to understand as being bad and deleterious and unpleasing – things like canned tuna, Donald Trump and Retford.

Bryson went to Retford for two reasons: because it is accorded capital letters on the British Rail route map, and because the *AA Book of British Towns* says absolutely nothing about it. 'Clearly,' Bill concludes, 'it was time to check this place out.' No, Bill. Clearly it wasn't time to check this place out. Clearly it was time to pay heed to the editorial team at the *AA Book of British Towns*, who by omitting Retford from their survey were probably trying to do us all a favour.

And so, a slave to prescription, I took a train to Retford. On the same journey two decades before, Bryson had the misfortune of sitting within earshot of a chap so smitten with his new mobile phone that he felt obliged to use it loudly and as often as possible; to clarify, for example, that he was still on the 10.07, was still due at Potato HQ at 13.02, and would most likely 'call again from Doncaster for no reason'. As I traversed the increasingly flat landscape of Cambridgeshire (much of which is below sea level; I'm told the fishermen need stepladders), I scanned the carriage for potato execs gabbing proudly on mobiles, but found only silent abusers, each bowed over their device – swiping right, scrolling down – as if in prayer.

On the edge of Retford is a place called Angelo's Bar, outside of which there is a board announcing that patrons who drink five pints will be awarded a sixth one for free, and that rooms are available upstairs, presumably with said patrons in mind. Inside, a dozen workmen in orange jumpsuits sat doggedly about the bar, waiting for something exciting to happen. I managed to speak with Angelo himself, who seemed to have taken advantage of his own promotion that evening. Angelo had no rooms available but said to try the Anchor Inn, which I did but to no avail. Once more finding myself in an unfamiliar town after dark with nowhere to stay, I entered a butcher's shop, where two kindly women put down their cleavers for a moment so they could search with bloody fingers for accommodation options on their smart phones. One of them made a customer wait five minutes while she scanned Trip Advisor. May they be rewarded in this life.

It appeared that my best bet was the Ivybrook, which I found without fuss: it sits just behind the main square, whose lining Georgian buildings Bryson had written favourably of. The central location of the Ivybrook is perhaps its single virtue, though one could argue that the further something is from the centre of Retford the better. Before issuing me a key, the owner of the guesthouse insisted that I sign the guestbook. Doing so, it became apparent that I was the first guest for six weeks. In spite of this fact, Steve was adamant that I kept him up to date as to my whereabouts, which I was to do by recourse to a wooden contraption fitted to the wall in the downstairs corridor. It was a sort of abacus, I suppose, with each sliding bead representing each guest. Every time I went out I was to slide my bead as far to the right as it would go, which I immediately had occasion to do when Steve invited me to the White Lion round the corner, where he conducts a weekly pub quiz. I entered the quiz and did miserably, at one point suggesting Humphrey Bogart to be the protagonist of a Tolstoy novel.

Afterwards, I took a double whisky at The Vine on Churchgate. A karaoke session had been scheduled for that evening and it was proving an effective deterrent. The MC – who was also the barman and a keen singer – didn't seem to care that he and I were alone in the bar and pushed on through a series of Roy Orbison songs. He did a particularly leftfield version of 'Crying'. I would like to say that there was something oddly satisfying about being alone in that empty pub with a double whisky listening to the barman cover Roy Orbison; something existential or poignant or character-building; something akin to the bittersweet darkness that runs through the novels of Camus and Sartre, and the darker songs of Johnny Cash and Billie Holiday; something like ennui, or a type of romantic self-loathing that forces a comprehensive revaluation of life and one's part in it, that tempts you to stab yourself in the hand with a butter knife just to see if it hurts – but there wasn't. It was simply and straightforwardly unsatisfying, and, unusually for me, the solitude made me lonely. I've always been good with my own company, but on this night I could have done with a paperweight, somebody to keep me from losing my place.

I stepped out onto the night streets of Retford, which were cold and ignored. Life, if it was happening at all, was happening indoors, behind net curtains and in front of television sets, each set giving news of mounting tension in Ukraine and the England captain's hamstring. There was a disappointed, ordinary stillness about the place, so little movement. Of course the shops were long shut, and of course the cold was proving a repellent, but where were those people moving from pub to pub, from pub to cinema, from restaurant to theatre, from theatre to home? Surely every town – especially a capitalised one – can manage a dozen such people? It was as if the evening had been cancelled and I was the only one spared the news. I had a decaffeinated coffee in a Wetherspoon pub, usually a busy franchise on account of the cheap beer and dinners. I spent five minutes stirring a single sugar into the coffee. The only sound, other than my turning spoon, was that made by a staff member emptying the ice-basins as she began to shut down the bar. It was just before ten o'clock.

I didn't sleep well. The heater in my room had two settings, on and off, the former contriving to bake anything within ten metres, the latter to freeze it. After a bracing shower, I went downstairs – drawn-out cartoon creaks – and found Steve waiting for me.

'You forgot to indicate that you were back in the building.'

'Did I?'

'You're supposed to move the bead across.'

'But you saw me come in.'

'It's about health and safety. I don't make the rules.'

'Should I change it now?'

'You'd better, really.'

'Actually, I'm going out now so we might as well leave it.'

'Two wrongs don't make a right.'

'Sorry?'

'Just change it now and then I'll change it once you're out.'

'You don't mind?'

'Not this once.'

The £17 room rate was meant to include breakfast, but neither of us mentioned it. Leaving, I wished Steve a merry Christmas, to which he gave a short laugh, as if the prospect were unlikely.

Retford was improved by the harsh morning sun, which put upon it a light glow that it seemed unsure how to wear. But even with the sun's help, and it being a Saturday, I wouldn't rush to call the town handsome or prosperous as Bryson had. I grant that most of the shops were at least occupied and open, but they were generally of the cheaper sort – pound shops, charity shops, second-rate retailers – with garish fronts decorated with handwritten special offers. I bought a brace of curd tarts from Bacon & Son on the high street. Mr Bacon told me that such tarts are particular to the region, which I consider a great shame, for they were excellent tarts, and ought to be ten-a-penny across the country.

I took the 42 bus to Worksop, a town of about 50,000 people situated on the northern edge of Sherwood Forest, where the legendary left-winger Robin Hood once carried out his own brand of fiscal reform. Since then, Worksop has evolved in a somewhat conventional fashion. First it received a charter from the King permitting a weekly market, which drew people to the town to live and trade. Over the next centuries, improved transport links (first the canal, then the railway) saw further expansion and commerce, and with them jobs and livelihoods. Then – and this is perhaps where Worksop's evolution differs from other towns – a good-looking local golfer called Colin took a seismic divot out of the fairway and uncovered a coal seam. For the next hundred years mining was the town's chief concern. By 1990, however, all the pits had been closed, because the government saw that it was cheaper, in the short term leastways, to get others to extract the coal and then buy it from them. But there were social consequences: Worksop experienced a period of high unemployment and drug abuse. Latterly, I'm told, things have picked up, and the town is now something of a hub for large-scale distribution: Wilkinson's, for example, are based here, and send out 15,000 six-inch rulers a week, according to one metric. There is also some light manufacturing, namely of beef stock cubes. Let us hope that particular industry doesn't dissolve as easily as coal mining before it.

Much of the above – the golfer, the stock cubes – I learnt in a pub near Worksop train station, where I stopped to see if I could stow my luggage. I had a considerable walk ahead of me – toward Welbeck Abbey – and I didn't fancy doing it with fifteen kilos on my back, so asked the landlady if I could keep my gear under the stairs for a few hours, which she agreed to so long as I bought a packet of crisps and a can of pop.

Bryson was mostly kind about Worksop, suggesting it to be an 'agreeable enough place in a low-key sort of way', and I'd say that just about still holds true. I was quite taken by the French Horn Hotel, which must have been some pub when it was still open, if only because of its gleaming tiles of olive and mint and caramel, which speak of a bygone era when public houses were small corner cathedrals, fetching communes to be proud of. In front of the pub, a pair of truants played penny-up-the-wall, drawing a small audience of elderly women as they competed for twenty-pence pieces. Their game – like the pub against which it was played – gestured to a time before plastic gadgets and Netflix. I gave one of the pair, who had just lost a coin down the drain after an anomalous ricochet, enough credit to keep the two of them out of school a while longer.

But I hadn't come to Worksop to regret the passage of time. I had come to visit Welbeck Abbey, a former monastery that since the 18th century has been the home of the Duke of Portland. (The fifth Duke, one W.J.C. Bentinck, is something of a hero of Bryson's, on account of his having been staggeringly unorthodox in his approach to life, but more of that anon.) At the south-western edge of Worksop I entered a residential area of large detached houses, the type Robin Hood might once have called on. Bryson mentioned a footpath hereabouts that runs all the way to the abbey, but I couldn't find it. At the top of Castle Farm Lane I stopped a Range Rover for guidance. The driver, in a tone that suggested a woman grown accustomed to directing young men, ordered me in. As I did as told, a dog no bigger than a Cornish pasty started yapping at the back of my head. 'Coco! Enough!' I asked the woman what all the land roundabout was exactly. 'It's ours,' she said, leaning across and opening my door for me.

Here are some of the ways in which W.J.C. Bentinck was unorthodox: he refused to talk to anyone, painted all his rooms pink, was an avid collector of wigs, blew a lot of cash on a subterranean mansion which required the employment of 15,000 men, and last but not least constructed a network of tunnels that allowed him to go jogging unseen.

I came upon one of these tunnels now, having been deposited by the Range Rover at the edge of a conifer plantation. Next to the tunnel's entrance was a small gatehouse, whose tenant told me that the tunnels had been blocked-off to stop teenagers from Mansfield running illegal half-marathons in them. I asked the man why Bentinck went to such lengths to keep a low profile, expecting to hear the usual tale of his being a committed and unerring aristocratic loon. Instead, he suggested that the duke commissioned the building of the ballroom and the network of tunnels less to appease his neuroses, and more to keep the local men in work. I prefer the former explanation.

Just about visible in the distance, if you cupped a hand and made a visor of it, was the minty roof of Welbeck Abbey. After passing through a large muddy field and crossing a small lake, I came to the abbey's gated back entrance. I noted its request to Stay Out and duly hesitated. Faced with a similar predicament, Bryson went for it, justifying his defiance by recourse to a strand of logic known as I've Come This Far So

You Can Get Stuffed If You Think I'm Turning Round Now. The abbey and its grounds were then a Ministry of Defence training centre, and as far as I was aware they still were, which added a certain frisson to my trespass. The gardens leading up to the abbey itself were unspectacular, and some of the shrubbery could have done with being cut back. Making a note of this in my journal, I was spotted by a patrolling security officer, who wanted to know just what I was up to. As Bryson before me, I was tempted to give my 'tourist-from-Iowa act', which I had rehearsed fastidiously on the train ('Someone told me I'd find some corn 'bout here'). Instead, I gave the excuse that I was searching for the golf course.

'The golf course?'

'That's right.'

'What do you want it for?'

To go ten-pin bowling for heaven's sake. 'To play golf.'

'I'd better give you a lift.'

'What?'

'I could drop you on the sixteenth. It's on my round.'

'You really needn't and I don't want to be any trouble and—'

'Come on! Jump in!'

It was hard getting back to the train station from the sixteenth. About four miles separate the two, and I walked each of them with a lowered head, biting into my scarf, thinking about the unhelpful decency of the security officer and my growing hunger.

I collected my backpack and then stamped my feet on the station platform waiting for the Lincoln train. As we rumbled in an old and empty carriage across the dark plain of Lincolnshire, I peered through misted windows at mysterious little stations. Around Gainsborough, I was taken by the slowly passing power stations, whose two-dozen chimneys, like so many upstanding cigarettes, gave a surreal smoke to the late crimson sky. It made for a beautiful prospect: the power, the palette of colours, the straight chimneys and the wayward smoke. Never, I don't think, have I been so drawn to a passing scene. Never have I pushed my face to a train window for so long. I was so drawn to the scene because I knew how transient and momentary its beauty was. If it can be reliably accused of anything, beauty is fugitive. It is but the quick harmony of random visual and mental elements – the smoke, the sky, the soft loneliness of evening train travel – and it stays still for no one.

It might have gone on forever that journey, for all I cared. It didn't of course. They never do. Journeys end, with or without our consent, with or without our knowing. I came to Lincoln.

16

Lincoln–Bradford

I knew little of Lincoln, but what I did know was in its favour: its cathedral was on a hill and it made sausages. Entering the city by train, you cut across a principal shopping street, forcing all sorts of traffic to a halt, and then pass a bright quayside, its edges laden with restaurants and cinemas and university buildings, each receiving and spitting out people. This brief composite – the people, the lights, the activity – suggested a city that goes on living after the six o'clock news has given its weather report; and, moreover, a city that goes on living no matter the content of that report, for on this evening the conditions were begging people to stay at home, and yet here they were, defiant and busy and gay. I felt a long way from Retford, and got off the train with a light heart, ready for anything.

I wanted to go immediately to the hilltop cathedral, but such were the conditions that it was impossible to sense where any incline might start. On leaving the station I went south on High Street and walked for about ten minutes, passing a dozen outlets purporting to do the best kebab in Lincoln, each one a clue that I was getting no closer to the city's Cathedral Quarter, with its Norman this and medieval that. That said, the revolving cylinders of meat, from which the best kebabs in Lincoln are drawn, might have been from any epoch, so indeterminate was their appearance.

I turned around and followed the road for half an hour until my calves were sore and I was unmistakably in another century. I was anxious, after Peterborough and Retford and Worksop, and the relative discomfort provided by those three, to have a bath and a decent bedroom, and so paid more than I could afford for a room at the White Hart Hotel. My room had a view of the cathedral, albeit across a jumble of ventilation shafts and fire exits. To get a better look of the cathedral, I climbed out of my window and onto the roof of the hotel kitchen, where I was subject to wafts of roasting pork and boiling veg. The cathedral was there all right. I looked up at it respectfully for a few minutes, as one might a renowned painting, vaguely impressed but not sure why. Behind one of the cathedral's high windows, the trickery of the stained-glass and the rain and the artificial light contrived to suggest a lone person stirring a pot of food.

After this flourish of sightseeing, I watched the news in the bath and reminded myself of what Bryson had got up to in Lincoln, in case I had a whole list of things to do that evening. I needn't have worried: Bryson had a quiet night, wandering the streets 'before and after dinner', and then turning in. I could manage that.

It is alleged you learn things by travelling. I have learned never to ask questions of people under 30. I had a beer at the hotel bar, where I failed to draw more than a sniff of personality from the young bartender. I am myself under 30, so I ought to be careful what I say, but it remains the case that the great majority of young people I have tried to engage on this trip have either been reluctant, preoccupied or witless. Perhaps I have just been unlucky with my sample group. Perhaps, sensing a likeness, I gravitate toward halfwits. Or perhaps young people are more deracinated – from their environment, from civic life, from the art of conversation – than ever before, on account of the technological changes that have made their graduation into adulthood a predominantly virtual experience.

I left the hotel and took to the streets, and what a fine set of streets they are, narrow and twisting and raked, so that one doesn't so much walk them as manage them. And when it is a little icy underfoot, as it was on this evening, one is ever calling at phone boxes and doorways to steady oneself. Bryson liked Lincoln because it was pretty and well preserved. The two qualities are not unconnected: Lincoln's prettiness owes to its being well preserved, and its being well preserved owes in part to the city going bankrupt about 500 years ago. As Lincoln's economy dried up, all further development was stalled. The city's medieval buildings – now venerated – were reluctantly left alone. As in the small historic Vietnamese town of Hoi An, whose river silted up and brought all commerce to a stop, Lincoln's beauty owes a debt to misfortune. Had its economy carried on growing, the city might have evolved into just another run-of-the-mill provincial town.

Ever since the Normans erected a castle on the city's summit, 'uphill' addresses in Lincoln have been an indicator of wealth and social status. Being of the aspirational sort, on leaving my hotel I continued upward, hoping to encounter a duke or duchess struggling to work a newspaper, or some posh young things on the terrace of a seafood restaurant, braving the cold in case the editor of *Tatler* happened to pass. Of course I saw no such things. For one, my understanding of the upper classes is crude and reductive – I am sure most are sensible, kind and altogether banal – and so it's unlikely I'd run into the fantastic cartoons of my imagination. And for two, the old dichotomy that positioned the well-to-do uphill and the rest of Lincoln downhill has buckled in recent decades. These days, no address is out of bounds for a lord.

Inch by inch, I lowered myself down Steephill. Outside the Strait and Barrow pub, which seemed busy and well enjoyed, I asked a man over 30 where I might find some music on this Saturday night. He recommended the Tap and Spile. I went and enjoyed some Blues for an hour. The four-piece band made quite a picture: big-boned Lincoln men, complexions reddened by wind and beer, calloused hands doing dainty things with strings and keys. Here were residents of Skellingthorpe and Nettleham and Washingborough singing about the ungovernable women of Mississippi and New Orleans. They were unmistakably down-to-earth men, men of this county, but their concerns, for a few hours at least, were exclusively with Venus.

There are only so many babies and sweethearts one can hear of without growing lonesome, and so I moved on to another pub, The Jolly Brewer on Broadgate, where there was music of an altogether different nature. An artist called Loop Cycle was engineering a piece of polyphonic electro-rock with his feet. He would take an instrument, produce a beat or riff, record it, play it on loop, and then add to it until the pub was host to an invisible orchestra. The composition wasn't as visceral and moving as the Blues, but it was impressive none-theless. Even more impressive was the cheese and pickle roll I purchased at the bar for £1.50. All pubs should keep such rolls behind the bar. The mature cheddar, the sweet pickle, the soft doughy roll, the half-pint of stout that I took with it, even the nostalgic unpeeling of clingfilm – all conspired to make an excellent dinner. Lincoln was being kind to me.

I continued downhill until my descent was blocked by a body of water. It was Brayford Pool, the quayside area I had passed on the train. During the Iron Age – whenever that was – a series of wooden dwellings were established next to this pool. Back then, the water would have reflected only elemental things: the moon, the stars, the sun. Now it catches the lights of Hollywood, whose new releases make bright surface con-stellations, and the neon names of chain restaurants. Passing trains are reflected as they go, and a file of keen eyes peer out onto the pool from the University of Lincoln's library. Said library is housed in a colossal warehouse which once dealt with tanks and munitions. Some feel that the expansion of the UK's Higher Education sector in the last decades is regrettable, but it is surely better that an edifice once busy building tanks to blow off heads is now, notionally at least, building better minds and futures.

You wouldn't guess it now but this whole area used to be manic with industry: locomotives, munitions, turbine engines, they were all put together on Lincoln's plain. As late as the 1950s, Lincoln was still a significant manufacturer, and its fac-tories and warehouses employed up to two thirds of the local working age population. Ever since, the city has seen a gradual decline in manufacturing, in sync with the changing economic profile of post-war Britain broadly, as the emphasis shifted from production to consumption.

Returning to the High Street, I passed another converted factory. This one used to build gas turbine engines; now it's a gymnasium. This struck me as a significant, and by no means exceptional, evolution of purpose. I can't decide whether such a shift – from the production of goods to the production of good looks – is for the better or not. I sometimes feel that if we – and I include myself in this 'we' – gave a tenth of the time we give to appearing good actually doing good, or nurturing ourselves in other, less superficial ways, we would be a finer (and no less fecund) civilisation. But who am I to say? I neither produce goods nor good looks. Both facilities – factory and gymnasium – find me wanting.

On the High Street a team of middle-aged men and women were issuing flip-flops to those who could no longer stand their heels. They were 'street pastors', and go about on Friday and Saturday nights not to preach but to issue support to those made vulnerable and disorientated by drink. The pastors were admirably non-judgmental when I asked if getting drunk to the point of violence and lechery and debilitation was a regrettable practice. They suggested that it was ever thus; that a working week, no matter its nature, can be a depleting and aggravating thing, and the instinct to forget about it for a number of hours was therefore understandable. The fallout from such attempts at forgetting – the altercations, the vulnerability – is what the street pastors are there to ameliorate. I was impressed.

And then Mick Townsend turned up. Addressing the team of pastors, of which he thought I was a member, Mick asked: 'Where were yous last night? I went down the underpass with food for the homeless but none was there. I was pissed off. I appreciate yous but yous wind me up, telling me the underpass and then no bugger's there. Yous have got to do more for the homeless.'

Mick was so wound-up by this point that he was genuinely scary. One of the pastors explained that the homeless weren't their only concern, that they were responsive to all kinds of vulnerability, explaining how, just the night before, he had helped a couple find their way home, neither of them being able to walk effectively. Mick didn't like this one bit.

'I hope you told him to man up.'

'No, I didn't do that,' said the pastor.

'If that bloke can't look after his woman he's gonna die, and you ought to let him. It's survival of the fittest, always has been. All the best civilisations were the ones that fucking survived. Vikings, Romans.'

'Yes and look what happened to those civilisations,' said the pastor.

'Yeah they fell, and you know what they fell to? Fucking democracy. All of 'em. And in ten years this country will too. We're too soft. It's gonna kill us. Too many fucking immigrants.'

And it was immigration that turned out to be Mick's preferred theme. His discussion of Darwinism and democracy had been just a warm up for a more pressing thesis, which, in short, was that immigrants are generally all right but they wind people up because they're different, which isn't a problem *per se* but becomes a problem when a country hasn't got the means or compassion or both to cope with that difference. Mick understood that – historically speaking – Britain was a country of immigrants, and that before the Indians or the Chinese or the Polish arrived the standard of living was worse than it is now, but, none-the-fucking-less, immigrants still wound him up.

Mick took a deep breath, and then sort of bounced on the spot for a while, as if getting ready to launch a final, unquestionable right hook. And then he came forwards and delivered his blow. 'Do you know the poet John Donne?' The pastor knew the name. 'No man, right, no man is a fucking island, and the bell, right, the bell ain't for no one.' And that was it. That was Mick done.

Breakfast wasn't included, so I made do with a foot-long Lincolnshire sausage from the Great British Cafe on The Strait, whose interior was decorated with all things commonly believed to capture the essence of British culture: The Beatles, Big Ben, Buckingham Palace – you get the picture. Mick Townsend was nowhere to be seen.

I ate my sausage passing through Temple Gardens, where I found the Usher Gallery, recently incorporated into a broader, award-winning institution called The Collection. Two things caught my attention in the gallery. The first was a young girl stood with her mother before a statue of Mars. The young girl drew her mother's attention to Mars's nakedness and asked why a god couldn't afford clothes. The mother, after a few seconds' thought, put forward a theory about the changing nature of social mores. The child, not thinking much of this, suggested a more straightforward explanation: 'And I suppose it is rather hot on Mars.'

The second thing was a painting of Lowry's. In 1932, Lowry had been commissioned by some of Lincoln's notables to paint the city. The commissioners evidently expected the cathedral to figure prominently in the painting, for they refused Lowry's initial effort, which included no trace of it. Lowry had opted to focus on the downhill exploits of the city's downhill people. The two parties reached a compromise, and the cathedral now has a spectral presence in the background of the painting.

Stirred by Lowry's portrayal of Lincoln, I had a mind to revisit the Great British Cafe and replace its Cool Britannia paraphernalia with images of relative poverty and unscrupulous politicians; add beef madras and jerk chicken and pierogi to the menu; and to introduce a policy of issuing credit to people with no hope of repaying. Only then would it be deserving of the title Great British Cafe. The tourists would love it.

I took a westward train through a series of dales to Bradford. I paid no heed to what passed by outside; I kept my face from the window and its motion picture. Instead, I recalled Bryson's claim that Bradford's 'role in life is to make every place else in the world look better in comparison', a claim he supports by citing the many closed shops, the TO LET signs, and the windows covered in 'posters for pop concerts in other, more vibrant communities like Huddersfield and Pudsey'. I'd been to

Huddersfield and from what I could remember its most vibrant feature is a statue of the former Labour Prime Minister Harold Wilson. Accordingly, I was tempted to pull the emergency brake and walk back to Leeds.

Bradford is at the junction of three valleys, among the foothills of the Pennines, and is bounded by high, open moorland. Arriving there, one feels immediately in another England. Indeed, it wouldn't have surprised or flustered me had the station manager asked for my passport. The city centre has something of the air of a filmset that has wrapped for the day, especially after dark. The fronts of the buildings might be so much plastic and woodchip, hiding cameras and changing rooms and lighting rigs, while the few people still scuttling around the streets might be the last of the extras – 'Difficult Customer', 'Woman on Bus', 'Unfriendly Milkman' – finishing up for the day. I can't imagine what sort of film they would be producing here. Perhaps a thriller set in a post-industrial dystopia, wherein the bitter ghosts of fallen factory owners prey on the wreck of the proletarian workforce; perhaps an updating of *Romeo and Juliet*, wherein Ahmed is banished from Yorkshire for daring to marry Leanne from Wakefield; or perhaps the sequel to the questionable, Bradford-based classic *Rita, Sue and Bob Too*, which, if the marketing team were earning their keep, would be called *Rita, Sue and Bob Too 2*.

It wouldn't be inappropriate if Bradford were a filmset. It is after all the first and only UNESCO City of Film, and home of the National Media Museum. It was this same museum that Bryson had come to Bradford for. On the afternoon of his visit, one of the museum's cinemas, the Pictureville, was showing a film called *This is Cinerama*. Bryson first saw the film as a toddler in Chicago in 1956, and was, to put it lightly, excited to see it again. I was unable to see the film, because it is no longer being shown once a month as it used to be. But perhaps that's no bad thing. From Bryson's description, the film sounds like a three-hour love letter to America. The climactic section of the film – an aeroplane flight over the United States set to 'a swelling stereophonic rendition of God Bless America' – just about sends the guy over the edge. With the credits rolling, Bill can be found stood on his seat calling for the reintroduction of military conscription, so the seeds of God Blessed America – liberty, democracy, macaroni cheese – can be sowed across the world.

No, I wasn't disappointed to miss out on *This is Cinerama*, not if I'm honest; but I thought I'd watch a film at the museum in any case, just to give my visit to Bradford some echo, some semblance, some deferential trace of Bryson's. In the Cubby Broccoli cinema – one of the museum's smaller screens – I saw *Nothing but a Man*, a 1964 film set in Alabama wherein the black protagonist's heroic resistance to white prejudice proves in vain – we leave him unemployed and unemployable and expecting a child. There were quite a few lone men in the audience, and many were part of Bradford's significant British-Asian population, whose first members arrived after the Second World War to apply their skills in the city's textile industry. In any case, the film seemed to strike a chord with its audience, albeit a solemn one. The travails of the protagonist were not unimaginable to many of those watching.

17

Saltaire–Harrogate

The average Brit consumes 40 litres of curry a year, if you can imagine it in such a form. Enoch Powell, in an infamous speech he gave in 1968 about the threats posed by multiculturalism, would have done better to warn of rivers of korma than rivers of blood. In 2012, for every roast dinner put on the table, over a hundred curries were shoved in the microwave. I wasn't being facetious when I said I'd add beef madras to the menu at the Great British Cafe in Lincoln.

Curry wasn't the gift of immigrants but the fruit of imperialism. When upper-crust Brits went abroad during the age of Empire, to plant flags and drink gin, they soon exhausted their supply of pork pies and black puddings and were obliged to sample the local fare. Not long after, Queen Victoria recruited a Bengali chef to run the kitchen at Osborne House. Then, in the 20th century, demobbed soldiers from the subcontinent, having fought patriotically for King and country, bought bombed-out London properties on the cheap and served curry through front windows, staying open well after the pubs had shut to make a few extra quid. So doing, they laid the foundations of a British institution – the curry house.

I mention all this because there are so many curry houses in Bradford that you could eat in a different one every week of your life. But I wouldn't advise that. I would take most of my meals at the Kashmir. The restaurant has an upstairs and downstairs. Upstairs the atmosphere is more formal. Downstairs, where the kitchen is, people sit at long plastic tables and the staff pay more attention to the cricket being shown on a small television on top of the fridge than they do the food and customers. Each time an Indian batsman hit a four or survived an lbw appeal, roars would go up in the kitchen, and the head waiter would dash off halfway through taking an order to confirm, as he suspected, that it was yet another adroit flick through midwicket. It was easy for some diners – those ignorant of the test match – to imagine that every five minutes or so something was going perfectly well, or perfectly wrong, with the lamb biryani. Notwithstanding the sudden collapse of India's middle order, the curry I had was very good, and the side portion of onion bhajis sufficient to feed any greedy slip cordon. The meal cost me under £6. I tweeted the fact.

Keen to walk off my dinner, I took a crabwise route through the area known as Little Germany, where Bradford's German and German-Jewish wool merchants once operated out of splendid neoclassical piles. Now, of course, there is not a German or a Jew or a German-Jew in sight – the First World War saw to that – and their once-proud, once-busy buildings are now each ripe for letting, just as they were in 1994.

I suppose it could be considered fortunate that the buildings of Little Germany stand at all, given how much of Victorian Bradford has been levelled. Most of the city's Victorian architecture was lost to the myriad 'planning insanities' that Bryson writes of: the modern office buildings and widened roads which together made mincemeat of Bradford's noble centre. Nonetheless, there is enough remaining of the city's heyday to suggest a once pre-eminent industrial town: St George's Hall, the old Wool Exchange, the Victoria and Midland Hotels: each would improve any street in Paris or Rome. I am no classicist, yet I often wonder if we will ever again routinely conjure such buildings as these, or if, as is probable, we will just carry on knocking them down like so many dominoes. Since Bryson's visit, however, both Forster House and Provincial House – massive modern eyesores built in the 60s – have been brought down by controlled explosion. Being an outspoken detractor of post-war urban development, it wouldn't surprise me to learn that Bill had turned up for the explosions, with a flask of coffee and a foldaway chair, wearing a T-shirt that said 'I Told You So'.

By the time I had considered these matters, Little Germany had gone and I was passing a remarkably large outdoor swimming pool. It was, I learnt, the principal element of Bradford's new City Park, contrived at a cost of 30-odd million and intended to put some life back into the town's civic heart. I have heard of some daft initiatives to revive ailing town centres, but the introduction of the largest outdoor water feature to Bradford's – which is in West Yorkshire, remember, where the average temperature is about eight degrees – is perhaps the daftest of the lot. Are the city's unemployed spinners and weavers and halal butchers all supposed to turn their hands to lifeguarding?

I carried on walking – Darley Street, Pitfall Street – and I don't remember feeling more alone at any point on my journey so far. It felt that I had the city to myself. I spoke with two patrolling police officers about the Bradford riots of 2001, whose participants were given wildly disproportionate sentences so as to deter others from acting likewise. A similar response from the State was seen after the London riots in 2011. In both cases, rather than addressing the underlying reasons for the outbreaks, the State's reaction was to punish those involved with unusual severity, a course of behaviour that only promises, I feel, to reinforce the underlying reasons.

Seeking stimulation, I entered the Ambassador Working Men's Club and found a karaoke session going on. I enjoyed the spectacle of a fierce-looking fellow doing a good job of Neil Diamond's 'Song Sung Blue', before doing a bad job, at the behest of his young daughter, of 'Wrecking Ball' by Miley Cyrus. The daughter, having given her commission, busied herself with crisps and texting, and paid little attention to her father's efforts to please her. I felt for the guy.

I ordered half a lager and immediately wished I hadn't. A couple of old boys at the bar laughed at me and told me to sod-off down south and finish my soft drink there. I finished my drink and ordered another half, which confused my new friends. 'If yous are going to 'ave a pint why 'ave it in bits, like?' I enjoyed that club, with its resident clowns reminiscing about the week before, when the same jokes were made and the same songs were sung, as the same empty city killed time outside. There was something of Bradford in that club, something brilliant and warm but sad also.

If Bradford's role is to make every other place seem better by comparison, I should like to see those other places. I believe a great many of them wouldn't be a patch on Bradford. There is the curry, for a start. The National Media Museum is splendid and affordable. The hills and moors that besiege the city are a time-old corrective to any quality of strife. And, let us not forget, there is the largest man-made water feature in the solar system, useful if you ever have 50 tons of potatoes to wash.

Yes, I wouldn't mind living in Bradford, all things considered. I could do worse than that. I could rent an office in Little Germany, the former quarters of some woolly magician, where I would come each day, with a bag of cheese and pickle rolls and a few bottles of stout, to scribble down my take on life. I could go out for curry at dinner time, see a film most evenings, and if no one else had a mind to walk the streets, I should have them to myself. I would do my best to make friends with the Bradford men and women – those 'big solid lumps of character' as Priestley calls them – who I reckon could teach me a thing or two, not least about my own shortcomings.

And I would read a lot of J.B. Priestley. That would keep the gloom at bay. Priestley was a Bradford boy, and in this chronicle I have quoted him more than any other writer, and I would have quoted him much more were it not for my allegiance to Bryson. Priestley died the year before I was born, and has a statue in the city. I went there now and thought: one statue is not enough; there ought to be one on every street, in honour of his *English Journey* alone, which, if I'm candid, is a far more precious and significant book than Bryson's, so crowded are its pages with humour and beauty and uncommon sense. The English people and their country have never looked so good and so bad as they do in Priestley's book. Perhaps, I thought solemnly, stood next to that one statue, perhaps I was following the wrong guy after all.

I stayed the night in the nearby village of Baildon. The parents of a friend of a friend live there, and were happy to put me up on one condition, that I broke one of their daughter's paintings and got toothpaste on the carpet.

After breakfast, my host Ian drove me down from Baildon to Shipley, which is a picturesque descent, and then up to Wrose, whence he pointed out a dozen mills that have been converted into this or that, and where I was able to appreciate for the first time the shapely topography and sad redundancy that characterises this part of the country.

Next we went to Undercliffe Cemetery, where former industrial heavyweights have been laid to rest. The headstones were properties in themselves, and grew in scale and pomp according to the date of the underlying's death, peaking in the early 20th century with one K.M. Pickleshort. Such is the size of the graves that there has been no room for newcomers since 1919.

From Undercliffe we drove down to Saltaire, where Ian showed me Salt's Mill, put up by wool magnate Titus Salt in the 1850s and now an art gallery and retail space. In its day, Salt's Mill was the biggest in Europe, covering nine acres, each square-metre a blare of raw, scolding and often fatal endeavour. When erecting the mill, Salt also built 850 cottages for his employees to live in, as well as a church and an institution for conversation and education. Importantly, Salt's model community had no pub, and the resultant combination of sobriety and intellectual advancement within the town would occasionally give its founder a headache. It wasn't unusual for a factory hand, having read a particularly risqué passage of Lenin or Marx, to go straight from the library to their master's office, determined to raise a few points on the matter of industrial relations.

The story of Salt and his mill certainly made a good impression on me, but nothing like as good an impression as the lunch I had in Saltaire, which was honestly one of the best value meals of my life. At an unassuming bakery I ordered a beef pie to take away. Following the local custom, and a tad anxiously, I had it drenched in mushy peas and mint sauce. It cost £1.02 and was indescribably delicious. I ate it as I walked through Roberts Park, and for the duration of that walk, and the duration of that pie, I was perhaps the happiest 27-year-old with few career prospects in the country.

At the edge of the park, and following Bryson's lead, I found the old tramway that runs up to Baildon Moor, where an amusement park used to set up each summer to provide the mill workers with a few thrills, as if the possibility of losing a hand at work any second wasn't thrilling enough. The park was forced to close a hundred years ago, after the odds of surviving the toboggan ride dropped from evens to 5/1 over the course of a summer.

From Baildon Moor I went looking for the ruined mansion of Titus Salt Junior, which I eventually found at the high end of a coppice. Milner Field was once one of the finest mansions in the country. Now it is but a few morsels of stone hiding beneath mud and foliage, a toilet for absentminded Labradors. I was starting to feel a bit like a Labrador myself, scurrying about in Bryson's footprints. The need to emulate another's tracks was spoiling my own. My journey had been reduced – or so it felt – to a string of boxes to tick.

So when I went to a nearby vantage point to look down on the Aire Valley, on its brown ribbons of hillside housing and its unlit chimneys and unmanned worksites and general air of lost prowess, I couldn't find the patience to wonder, as Bryson had, what old Titus Salt would make of it all. And I didn't wonder, as Bryson had, what all those people in all those houses did with themselves now that the wool had been pulled over their eyes and from under their feet, now that the mills were flats or galleries or dust, now that those brown ribbons of hillside housing, built to service a particular industry, no longer had that industry to serve. And nor did I care much, for whatever all those people in all those houses were doing, they were surely better off than their forebears. When this part of the world was at its industrial peak – during its so-called 'heyday' – those chimneys kept the local life expectancy at eighteen.

By now it was cold and dark, and I had no idea where I was going to stay that evening. I knew it ought to be in Harrogate, but where exactly? I couldn't hope that the richest town in the north would have a youth hostel, and it was too late to consider couch-surfing. In the cafe at Bingley train station, I started making calls to the better hotels in Harrogate. After all, if you are going to blag something, it might as well have five stars.

As I paid the taxi driver on the forecourt of Rudding Park Hotel, Harrogate, a bellboy came to the window, hoping to assist with my designer suitcases. But I had only a muddy backpack that had two bananas escaping a side pocket. Somewhat embarrassed, I tried to refuse his service, but he insisted and took my bag from me, before struggling to carry it in a way that both suggested my importance and concealed the fruit.

It being a Monday out of season, and my being an established writer with a significant book on his important hands, I was put in the bridal suite. I hadn't had a proper wash for a few days, so I thought I'd have a go in the bath, which took an hour to run, such was its size. I put the television on and climbed in, but I was premature in doing so, for the water and bubbles still only covered my ankles and bottom, obliging me to keep the tap running, with the result that I could no longer hear Nigella Lawson saying something poetic and suggestive about meringue peaks, which was a shame, for isn't Lawson's voice one of the chief reasons one watches her cooking shows, in the bath or otherwise? Indeed, so well does Nigella enunciate certain words that the suite's voice-activated lighting system threw me into a blackout when she mentioned a dark chocolate mousse.

Newly restored, I went down to the bar to order the only drink I could afford. Given that I was in the bridal suite, it was somewhat confusing to encounter a wedding reception in full swing. I couldn't help fearing there had been a mistake, and that the married couple were presently consummating their vows in a single room with no view.

I went to bed but struggled to get comfortable. The various quilts and sheets and tapestries were so tightly tucked under the mattress that even some fierce kicking and writhing failed to issue any slack, with the result that I was unable to sleep on my back as per my custom without snapping a metatarsal. I honestly thought about phoning down for a sleeping bag.

It has been suggested that Harrogate is the happiest place to live in the UK, which is patently untrue. The passengers who rode the bus into town with me the next morning did so with apathetic expressions, and as they alighted they each gave a tremendous sigh, as if they were stepping into the very fires of hell. In fact, they were stepping onto Station Parade, whose collection of shops didn't, it must be admitted, seem the type to induce happiness, consisting as they did of a pawn shop, a betting shop and a provider of emergency cash loans at high interest.

On Cambridge Street I spoke with a *Big Issue* vendor about Harrogate being a happy place, and he knew something about what I was referring to. It had been discovered, he told me, that the citizens of Harrogate drink alcohol to hazardous levels and watch pornography more than any other set of citizens. Some opportunistic blogger then disingenuously extrapolated from these findings that Harrogate's people must, ipso facto, be our kingdom's happiest, when in fact they are probably some of the saddest. I have watched porn and I have drunk to hazardous levels, and I have never emerged from the experience feeling anything but miserable.

The *Big Issue* magazine is mostly sold by the homeless. It costs £2 and the vendor keeps half of that. The vendor I spoke with wasn't homeless; he has a small council flat in Knaresborough, and earns enough from selling magazines ten hours a day to tick over, with some support from the council to pay the rent. He could, of course, have been on the dole, but that wouldn't do for him, for he needs to be active. 'It keeps you in the game,' he said, 'stops you from losing it'.

The vendor pointed out three Romanians further along the street, who alternate between playing the accordion and selling the magazine. I asked if he minded the competition. 'Some do, but not because they're Romanian. Same with anything – if too many people are flogging the same thing, it gets testy. Besides, I'll always earn more because I'm a local boy and I've got the chat.' And he did have the chat, well and truly, and so we went on chatting until I asked whether our chatting was affecting his trade and he said that it probably was if he was honest.

I went to Betty's, where Bryson took his wife for a slice of cake. I had been warned that Betty's was a bit posh, which didn't altogether surprise me, given the history of Harrogate. After medicinal waters were discovered here in the 16th century, rich people started coming to make use of them. Accordingly, much of the town's architecture and parks have an air of Victorian grandeur: bold, opulent, well-kept. As with most single-industry economies, however, trade soon slowed down, particularly after it was discovered that iron-rich water does nothing for broken ankles.

But Harrogate learnt a new trick: it became a commercial, conference and exhibition hub. During the Second World War the government did much of their business here, preferring the flowers and cream teas of Harrogate to the falling bombs of London, and ever since then the town has been *the* place to have get-togethers. The Eurovision Song Contest was even held here in 1982, if you'll credit that. The whole of the BBC's broadcast can be found on YouTube. The opening footage shows a map of Europe with the question 'Where is Harrogate?' emerging in different languages from each of the competing countries. This is followed by some footage of the town's defining features, like Betty's tearoom, and the state-of-the-art Harrogate Centre, and a room of happy people watching pornography.

Back in 1994, Bryson informs us that the staff at Betty's were still in the habit of wearing frilly cotton caps. Alas, they do so no longer. I suggested to one of the staff that I had only come for the hats, to which she replied that there were websites for that sort of thing. (And she, being a woman of Harrogate, ought to know.) All of the confections looked a bit too precious for my taste, so I made do with a couple of samples before tracking down the *Big Issue* vendor and offering him the money that I would have spent on raspberry macaroons.

Waiting for my train to Leeds, where I would change for another to Manchester, I recalled Bryson's remark about the often-shocking degrees of inequality appreciable in the north of England. For Bryson, the imbalance makes the region 'a much more interesting place'. I suppose the inequality might well appear interesting for those benefitting from it, but I won-der how interesting it is for those at the wrong end of things. One of the problems with social inequality is that it's hard to know who to blame for its existence. There isn't a group of fat cats pulling the strings so that only a few do well and the rest do not. Inequality – of means, opportunity, life expectancy – isn't an executive decision. It is mostly systematic and self-perpetuating. If it is going to be addressed effectively then the grass roots have to be treated. That's why education is so important. There should be no private education for a start, and I don't care how uninteresting that is. Then something has to be done to negate the effects of nepotism, that entirely reasonable instinct to give a foot-up or helping hand to people we know. When Nick Clegg, then deputy Prime Minister, suggested illegalising nepotism in the House of Commons not a single member didn't roar with laughter.

The American dream – that anybody from any walk of life can rise to the top and acquire what they wish – is fallacious. The British Dream is not dissimilar. We hear a lot about social mobility these days, about equality of opportunity. Our meritocracy, they say, justifies our inequality. But that's all fallacious, too. The child of a doctor or lawyer or someone else in a professional position is twenty times more likely to get a job of equal status than the child of a waitress or parking attendant. Either the talk of social mobility is just that – talk – or the devices being employed to foster it are proving wildly ineffective. And it will get worse before it gets better. The more privatised the country becomes the more handicapped is any government that wants to create a fairer society. Education is becoming more privatised not less. Nepotism is becoming more rank not less. Barriers to opportunity – tuition fees, unpaid internships – are becoming more formidable not less. No, it would require a revolution, and seeing as the least well off in this country either have just enough not to be viciously frustrated, or too little time to proactively counter the nation's socio-economic narrative and ideological direction, a revolution appears unlikely. I'm not going to start one, because I don't care enough. But I do care enough to know that inequality isn't interesting, in the north of England or otherwise.

And with that I went to Manchester.

18

Manchester–Wigan

The short train journey to Leeds was the best I've had since riding through Siberia in winter. The carriage – for there was only one, though it made the noise of ten – rode along a low shelf between hills, with only postcard colours and scenarios on either side, each made better by the sun. It was a different kind of beauty to Bradford's, which is a harsh, emotive sort; here the beauty was typical, clichéd even, the work of a pastoral water-colourist under commission, painting for the textbooks, as if asked to portray the genre itself.

And yet people ignored it, preferring to text and swipe and share and like, as if beauty were only available online. The passengers' indifference to the beauty about them reminded me of a time in Tenerife when Aphrodite herself laid a beach towel five metres from my own. I turned to an old friend and told him that, were Aphrodite to ask for my phone number with a view to marriage, I would refuse her, explaining how it would be a tragedy to grow accustomed to such beauty, for it to grow cold, for it to slowly and imperceptibly lose its lustre. He laughed then and he laughs now.

Manchester is no Aphrodite. She is no beauty at all. Her looks aren't helped by the weather, of course, which is the stuff of jokes, and nor were they helped by the Blitz, which accounted for much of the city's historic centre. Not that Manchester was especially beautiful before the Luftwaffe visited. At the height of its import in the early 20th century, having grown mighty on a diet of cotton, Manchester was known as the Warehouse City, which tells you rather a lot. Now, the cotton having snapped, those warehouses are empty or rubble, which tells you even more.

To be fair, some of the city's central areas have been spruced up of late: Salford Quays now has the BBC and The Lowry Centre and innumerable shiny apartment blocks; the canals and viaducts at Castlefield have been renewed; and at Spinningfields, the super-glassy shopping precinct behind Deansgate, one can finger Versace and Armani before standing trial at the adjacent crown courts.

But that is Manchester. What of Greater Manchester, that vast urban zone stretching from Rochdale to Bolton, nearly every acre of which was once employed in the dirty process of cotton? In short, it's not a picture of health. When the cotton industry choked on its own smoke and died, its wake was long and ugly and could be seen in all directions. It was too panoramic to repair. You can't spruce up a thousand square kilometres.

I lived through that jokey weather and among those bad looks when I studied in Manchester a few years ago. I lived on the Oxford Road, a clove's throw from Rusholme and its famous Curry Mile. I was studying contemporary literature, and at that time Martin Amis was the celebrity member of staff in the English department. By all accounts it cost the university an arm and a leg to get Amis on board (several of each in fact, for half-a-dozen professors were forced to make room for him). The idea, I suppose, was to make the department more attractive to potential students.

I say students but perhaps I would do better to say customers, for ever since the effective termination of state funding of Higher Education in 2012, and the consequent introduction of £9,000 tuition fees to make up the shortfall, that is in essence what the students have become. Without the students' custom, Manchester University (and its humanities departments in particular, which don't get the research investment that other departments do), would be at risk of closure. So, in a bid to make the institution more appealing, in came Martin Amis and sushi and beanbags. From what I remember, incidentally, Amis's contribution to the department amounted to fortnightly sermons, wherein he would reminisce about that lunch he once had with Balzac in Paris. Amis has since left Manchester, having accepted a five-year contract with the LA Galaxy.

Manchester, then, wasn't new to me; I knew one or two things about the place; I knew the buses of Oxford Road, the tiles of the Arndale, the rum characters of Hulme and Moss Side. And yet, were someone to ask me to describe the place, I would find it difficult to do so. Perhaps Bryson was right when he said that Manchester lacks distinguishing features. There is, after all, no castle or bridge or Big Ben. The buses aren't red, and neither are the phone boxes. The architecture is a mash of styles – gothic, neoclassic, brutalist – which although a pleasant kind of disorder can make putting your finger on Manchester difficult.

In place of such iconic signifiers – castle, bridge, Big Ben etc. – are plenty of subtler things that define and recommend the place: the Royal Exchange Theatre, The Midland Hotel, the trams, Uncle Thomas's Chop House (and its corned beef hash especially), the surrounding countryside (the Lakes, the Peaks, Snowdonia), the Northern Quarter, the Bridgewater Concert Hall, the 80,000 students, and Wigan Athletic Football Club.

None of these things are apt to appear on a postcard, or at the centre of an Olympics bid, but they are all fine things nonetheless. Moreover, the father of Friedrich Engels had a factory in Manchester during the Industrial Revolution. Engels invited a friend – one Karl Marx – to come and take a look at it. Marx probably wrote chunks of *Capital* on the Curry Mile. That is enough for me. There is Manchester's postcard.[5]

Manchester also has *Coronation Street*, of course. Back in 1994, Bryson took a tour of the Granada Studios where the soap opera is filmed, and enjoyed (to an unreasonable degree) peering through net curtains and learning which characters had recently drowned in the bath. I couldn't follow suit because Granada stopped doing tours fifteen years ago, which was a shame because although not an avid watcher of the show I had been reading about it and wouldn't have minded a glance behind the scenes.

Most of all I would have liked to have seen the house of Ken Barlow. I have developed something of a soft spot for Ken. When the show first screened in 1960, young Ken, having won a university scholarship, was getting a load of grief off his dad for becoming posh – not something one easily gets away with in Manchester. After graduating Ken thought he'd let his hair

---

[5] Yes, I know Manchester wouldn't have had a curry mile in the middle of the 19th century.

down and get married, only for his wife to electrocute herself with a hairdryer. After 634 episodes in mourning Ken emerged from the ashes of his grief to marry Deirdre, only for Deirdre to start an affair with Mike Baldwin within a fortnight. A year or so later, just to rub salt in the wound, Baldwin would proceed to marry Ken's daughter. Given the amount of strife Ken went through in Manchester, it's a wonder he never thought to skip town.

There aren't streets like Coronation Street anymore. The bricks and mortar may still be there but the way of life that *Coronation Street* represents – the camaraderie, the interdependence – has crept away, I feel. And perhaps that's no bad thing. Here, after all, was a place where dogs fell in the canal, where murder and infidelity and freak traffic accidents occurred three times a week for 50 years. During the 70s and 80s more people died on Coronation Street than at the hands of the Irish Republican Army. The trams are liable to derail, people give birth in the pub, every other resident has been in prison, and the local factory is called Underworld, for heaven's sake.

Coronation Street the programme is going nowhere, however. In fact, Granada has just built a new set near Salford Quays, next to the Imperial War Museum. The set is built to full scale, rather than three quarters as the old one was. Ken Barlow, I'm told, is now over seven-foot tall. And there is now even a *Coronation Street* video game, wherein you play the role of a detective trying to solve some new piece of nastiness that's hit the fan. I would interview Ken first. I would take him to the Rovers Return (if he still fits inside) and buy the guy a drink. Boy, does he deserve one.

After arriving at Manchester Victoria station, I went to a favourite bar called Big Hands on the Oxford Road, where I hoped to get a sandwich and some strong coffee and maybe do a little writing. I got talking with a literature PhD student called Rupert, who told me all about his research, which had to do with Jane Austen being a diabetic. Academic projects of this sort – *Jane Austen was a Diabetic*, by Rupert Goodness-Gracious – do seem dangerously niche. Perhaps it's the collective impact of such research projects – the dragging of knowledge along a few metres – that justifies each individual effort, however parochial. A few years ago, I was about to start my own PhD in Manchester. I wanted to look at Shakespeare's use of frozen food as a dramatic device, but pulled out at the last minute, believing there to be some better way to spend my life. If I'm frank, I'm still looking for that better way.

Upon Rupert's invitation, I attended a lecture at the university entitled The Great University Gamble, which intended to outline the inherent risks in remodelling Higher Education in England along American, neo-liberal lines. That intention was not met, alas, for the lecture failed to go ahead. The overhead projector, you see, refused to play ball, which made it impossible for the speaker to deliver his presentation. I later learned that the overhead projectors at the university are now programmed not to work after 6 as a cost-cutting measure, made necessary by the new, austere economic climate in which university departments are forced to operate. The lack of a lecture on The Great University Gamble on account of the great university gamble seemed to me as effective an illustration of the perils ahead as anything the speaker might have offered. So it goes.

I had time to go and see the infamous Arndale Centre before taking a bus to Wigan. In the 1960s, it was decided by the city's councillors that the jumble of shoddy Victorian streets between Piccadilly Gardens and Corporation Street were hopelessly inadequate for the modern shopping public. What was needed, it was felt, was a vast monstrous indoor shopping centre that would prove so expensive to construct that each of the companies involved in its development would end up bankrupt.

The developers were unashamedly and openly in thrall to American trends. If this wasn't ominous enough, they were also adamant that they wanted the Arndale Centre to offer very little natural light and for its exterior to be covered in urine-coloured tiling rather than shop frontages – hence the Arndale's famous lavatorial image. The architects warned the developers that this would create a very introverted and very unattractive building. They were ignored.

Despite the mounting criticism levelled at them, the developers maintained that they were building the finest shopping centre in the world. They did no such thing. When completed, the Arndale was widely considered to be Europe's ugliest shopping complex and became one of Britain's least-loved buildings.

The IRA evidently disliked the place, for it bombed the Arndale in June '96, in the biggest ever terrorist attack on British soil. On the morning of the attack, a van containing a 1,500-kilogram bomb was parked between Marks and Spencer and the Arndale. A coded message was sent to the Granada Studios, warning of an imminent explosion. The area was evacuated and a bomb squad was called in from Liverpool, but to no avail. (The bomb squad, incidentally, was late arriving on account of a faulty train. Have you ever heard of a bomb squad arriving by train?) 1,200 properties on 43 streets were either ruined or damaged. Despite there being no fatalities, the damage was enormous, and forced a comprehensive regeneration of Manchester's commercial centre. It surely wasn't their intention, but the IRA did Manchester a favour.

I took a double-decker bus and travelled northwest through endless streets that 'never seemed to change character or gain any'. As if caught in a benign coma, the streets of Eccles and Atherton were still dotted with garages, hairdressers, brick shopping precincts and betting establishments. There were signs of an emerging cosmopolitanism, however. The parade of shops at Tyldsley, for example, consisted of Kebab King, Sol-Tan, William Hill and Hung Wing. It would be hard to imagine a more British quartet.

On his bus ride to Wigan, Bryson passed the time reading Orwell's *The Road to Wigan Pier*. Neither Orwell nor Bryson had much hope for Wigan upon their respective arrivals, so stubbornly beleaguered is that town's reputation. After visiting, Orwell still had no hope, and quickly set about saying as much. Bryson however found the place to be handsome and well-maintained, not least because of its new shopping arcade – The Galleries – which had been deftly integrated into a row of commercial buildings in a fashion that was both contemporary and respectful of the contiguous buildings. To celebrate this architectural feat, Bryson had a sticky bun and a cup of tea at the Corinthia Coffee Lounge, where he made the mistake of asking someone under 30 what a Georgian Potato Oven is exactly. 'It's for cooking potatoes and tha'".

There would be no sticky bun for me, however, because the coffee lounge had recently shutdown, The Galleries having lost a lot of its trade to an even newer shopping arcade across the road, which had successfully if pointlessly shifted Wigan's shoppers from one building to another. Do these restless developers imagine that by building more shops the population of a town – that is, the number of shoppers it can put forward to spend and browse at any one time – will miraculously double? Through the grubby windowpanes of the former Corinthia Coffee Lounge I saw upended Formica-topped tables and chairs marked with lot numbers, ready for auction. It was actually quite sad to see.

Wigan is renowned for something other than social deprivation – pies. The town hosts an annual pie eating competition, and the average Wiganer is thought to consume over 250 pies a year. I went to a place called Bruciano's and ate a plate of steak pie, mushy peas, chips and gravy. The proprietor was a stout woman who used to play rugby league for St Helens, and during this busy lunch hour she seemed to be performing half-a-dozen tasks at once (buttering, portioning, calculating), all the while keeping up a salty stream of consciousness about the weather, sandwich fillings and the governing coalition. The atmosphere in the cafe was boisterous and good-humoured – an atmosphere that I would come to recognise, over the next week or so, as decidedly Lancastrian. Most of the customers were well over a hundred years old, and they each had something to say for themselves. One gentleman, manifestly disappointed with his lunch, repeatedly announced in a loud flat tone to no one in particular that his pie was 'nowt but gravy'. The cafe was not formed in 1907 as a plaque suggested. 'That's there just to give the *impression* of age,' said the proprietor. I told her that such subterfuge was plainly unnecessary.

I went next to Wigan's covered market, where one can rent a stall for £90 a week, and where genuinely useful things are sold, as opposed to the new, well-heeled sort of markets that only seem to do balsamic vinegar and duck eggs. There was a rum cast of stall holders, each looking larger than life, like down-to-earth cartoons. Some were absorbed in a book or a crossword; others wandered the aisles with a cup of tea and a look of amused, sagacious cunning. The gentleman who thought little of his pie was busy selling comic books and antique dictionaries. I roamed around fingering corkscrews and pork pies and hard-boiled sweets. I bought a bag of Joe's Mint Balls, of course.

The new shopping arcade, which I took a look at, is far more spacious than the old one, and poorer for the fact. It seems especially designed to prevent casual interactions, as if the architect had been tasked to make shopping a strictly contactless sport. This seems all wrong to me. Do we really want so much room to ourselves – at home, at work, at the shops, on holiday – that the chance of social encounters is expunged? Are we really that prim and taciturn? I don't think so. Were a public consultation undertaken, I'm confident its findings would show a preference for intimacy and conviviality and neighbourliness over isolation and distance. And yet so much contemporary thought and practice – by government, by big business, by developers – actively, and often well-meaningly, works and lobbies to deny us such things. Privacy has been made into a fetish, and now it is for us – the dutiful citizen, the dutiful consumer – to crave it uncritically.

Wigan is made more attractive by its hill. The climbing and falling streets, with their leaning half-timbered buildings, seem to throw and drag their traffic about, and the town's uneasy rooflines contrive to suggest character and gaiety and whimsy. In spite of the weather, which was really quite bad by now, the streets had an avuncular quality – homely, benevolent, a little bit queer.

Having nothing better to do, I took the road to Wigan Pier. There seems to be perennial uncertainty as to what exactly Wigan Pier is, or was, or might be. Some, like Paul Theroux and Orwell, say it is nothing at all, that it was demolished long ago. Bryson says it is an old coal shed, recently turned into a museum. I was told, on the other hand, that it was 'nowt but decking' – a tiny wooden jetty where coal was once dropped off. I could easily have found a definitive answer – a few clicks on my phone would have done the job – but I preferred the uncertainty.

There is no mistaking Trencherfield Mill, however, which sits across from what might or might not be the pier. It was a working mill at the time of Bryson's visit but has since been converted into apartments and a cafe – a typical shift of purpose, and one that I have learnt not to begrudge or regret.

As Bradford, Wigan is probably cleaner and better for having lost its old industry. At one point, 90 per cent of Wigan's workforce mined coal, and there were a thousand mine shafts in the town – one for every five people. The money produced by this mucky work, of course, had the habit of skipping town at the first opportunity. No, I'm glad the mines are gone, I'm glad this old mill is now apartments and a cafe. Let them eat cake if the pies run out.

At Wigan North Western railway station they have removed all the poems. I'd visited the station a few years earlier, and had enjoyed reading the poetry on the platform and in the waiting room. It wasn't your flowery sort of poetry, and it wasn't obscure either. It was good, unpretentious stuff, and it made the act of waiting more bearable. But now they were gone. Just why would you do that?

One other person was waiting for the delayed service to Liverpool Lime Street. He asked me what I was up to with such a large backpack. I told him I was travelling about the country. 'Why?' he said. 'For no good reason,' I said. He nodded approvingly and then told me that he was waiting for a girl called Ashley to arrive. He'd only met her a few times. Was going to take her out for an Italian meal. Would probably snog her face off at some point in the evening. Then his phone rang – it was Ashley – and all thought of snogging her face off seemed to escape his mind, for all he could manage was to ask very sweetly and timidly whether she was okay and whether her train was on time. When her train finally arrived, and Ashley stepped off, the man was barely able to look at his date. He was obviously and incurably smitten, and Ashley didn't look entirely indifferent either. I watched the two of them climb the steps to leave the station, he offering to carry her bag, she saying don't be daft it's just a bloody handbag, he laughing nervously, she with real affection. Maybe Wigan North Western hadn't lost its poetry, after all.

19

Liverpool

After arriving at Liverpool Lime Street station, I went first to the Adelphi Hotel, refuge of Bryson in '94 and Priestley in '33. The hotel was built to serve the first-class ferry passengers en route to New York. It must have been a grand hotel once, when there was sufficient trade and confidence to keep the whole place looking like a million dollars. Now there is less trade and less confidence – these days the ferries go to Birkenhead and Cork, not New York and Zanzibar – and the hotel is all fur coat and no knickers. Remembering that Bryson had fallen down the stairs here, I went inside and asked if anyone remembered an unwieldy American making a prat of themselves. I was encouraged to be more specific, on account of that sort of thing happening several times a week.

Lime Street itself is a useful introduction to the city. Its Irish pubs point to the historical relation between Liverpool and Ireland, which peaked in the 1840s when two million Irish, made desperate by famine, came here either to settle or to take a boat to America. The street's buildings are a telling mix of Victorian pomp and flaky post-war pragmatism and point to the vicissitudes that have shaped the city over the past 300 years: the slave trade prosperity; the recessions of the 1920s and 1980s; the bombs of the Luftwaffe. Already, then, I was being drawn to the city's buildings, despite having told myself to focus on its people (are *they* derelict? are *they* pragmatic?).

But people are much harder to stare at. Buildings don't tend to move, for a start, and rarely mind being picked over.

At either end of Hope Street is a cathedral – one Catholic and one Anglican, the latter a red-brick monster, the former a giant kitchen appliance, a blender built on a biblical scale. The Hope Street Hotel is housed in a former carriage works and fire station, which date to the 1860s. An atmosphere of conversion, of tasteful, creative updating, runs throughout the hotel: lacquered wood, decorative shards of glass, baked beans served in espresso cups. From the window of my hotel room, across so many Georgian chimneys, I could see most of the city – the radio tower, the Mersey, the Royal Liver Building. I was tempted to climb out as I had in Lincoln and make for the Three Graces. Instead, I had a bath and listened to a Scouse DJ on the radio saying something about the state of Steven Gerrard's ankle.

I needed to drink five pints of beer and find a Greek restaurant. Bryson had the bulk of those pints at The Philharmonic Dining Rooms so that he could use the toilets there, which are said to be the nicest in the country. I wouldn't know, for I didn't need to go, and didn't much fancy heading in to pretend.

I found Bryson's Greek restaurant – Zorbas – at the foot of Hardman Street. When Bryson ate here he got so drunk that he threatened to buy the business, before leaving a tip of 'such lavishness as to bring the whole family to the kitchen door'. I opted for the moussaka, and it was excellent. I had a Cypriot beer with my meal, which reminded me of a sculpture in the gardens of Clare College, Cambridge. I like how that can happen, how a beer in Liverpool can evoke a sculpture in

Cambridge; how by travelling we develop our web of associations. From now on, each time I add salt to my food I shall think of Titus and his mill and his statue overlooking the cricket field. Each time I read John Donne I shall think of Mick Townsend in Lincoln. And each time I hear a plaintive trumpet I shall think of the *Coronation Street* theme tune and the travails of Ken Barlow. Sensibility is one of the unheralded fruits of travel.

In the morning, after some poached eggs and a double shot of baked beans, I went down to the river. High, shiny buildings seemed to be going up everywhere. The view from my hotel room was now engulfing me, each building now inviting – nay, demanding – individual respect and consideration, as if annoyed to have been squashed the night before into a lazy cityscape. From my window these buildings had the look of toddlers. Now I saw that they were no toddlers at all, but a muscular crowd of boastful adults, exiled from the skyline of New York.

Respectful of Bryson's example, I rode a ferry on the Mersey. On account of the wind, it was near impossible to make sense of the on-board historical commentary. But I knew enough already. I knew that Liverpool was once the third-richest city in the British Empire, that it sent its first ship to pick up slaves in 1699, that rum and cotton and tobacco and palm oil once passed through these docks and through these streets as freely and abundantly as oxygen. I also knew that on top of trading, the Liverpool of yesteryear was also busy pioneering. The city was pregnant for a century, it seems, and gave birth to half the modern world: the first council house, the first railway, the first free school meals, the first repertory theatre, the first skyscraper, the first financial derivatives and the first hair extensions. Allen Ginsberg, the beat poet, said that Liverpool was 'the centre of consciousness of the human universe'. Even if he was wrong, his estimation is telling.

Of course things changed. Trade slowed, ships berthed, ideas dried up and slaves went out of fashion. There was a period of sclerosis, when Liverpool was forced to reflect and fight and adapt. In one generation – between 1966 and 1985 – it went from the country's second-busiest port to being quieter than Grimsby and Hartlepool. One hundred thousand livelihoods were lost on the wind. And yet, says Bill, when you are in Liverpool 'you still feel like you are some place'. Well, you feel that even more now.

I tend to be sceptical of the term 'regeneration', which implies that something degenerate needs fixing, which isn't always the case; but about Liverpool's regeneration I am not sceptical. There are hands on deck in Liverpool, and they are plainly working with dexterity and confidence and a pleasing measure of bombast. They are also plainly working *up to a point*. From the Mersey it is easy to see how the regeneration stops abruptly at the Tobacco Warehouse in the north and the Baltic Triangle district in the south. Liverpool might not be a paradise just yet, but it has certainly got out of the blocks well enough.

Back on dry land, I went to the Merseyside Maritime Museum. A few things have stayed with me from that museum, mostly to do with the sinking of the Titanic. I remember Bruce Ishmay, chairman of the White Star shipping line, who jumped desperately into one of the final lifeboats and was ever after considered a coward. I remember the quartet of musicians who played on heroically (or inattentively) as their socks grew soggy. And I remember a section of the museum that was concerned with camp sailors (KAMP: known as male prostitute), for whom the early P&O ferries were a sort of refuge, a place of tolerance where orthodox prejudices were unofficially suspended. The sailors even used a dialect of their own – Polari – which allowed them to commend a pair of bijou sallies without drawing attention.

Above the museum is the new, and belated, International Slavery Museum, which contains many stirring and sobering testimonies of Britain's lamentable involvement in the Atlantic Slave Trade. The vast and complicated legacy of this includes the Toxteth riots of 1981, when certain members of Liverpool's Toxteth community (black *and* white) let their feelings be known about the discriminatory practices of the police.

I walked south along the river with the loose intention of finding the Baltic Triangle, an area of the city where several defunct warehouses have been converted into the sort of hip cafe-bars that play vinyl records, hang bikes on the wall and serve cutting-edge sandwiches. Halfway along King's Parade I stopped to consider the water. The sun was setting now, giving Birkenhead the look of a town patiently ablaze, with calm banks of flame pushing outward from its middle-class square before losing heart and turning slowly blue, black, purple over Tranmere. The estuary had grown shy, its water receding to expose long flats of wet sand, upon which a lone gull walked back and forth like a boatswain.

I came to the Baltic Triangle. At the corner of Upper Parliament and Jamaica Streets (and what a co-ordinate that is, by the way) the lights of a cafe-bar shone beckoningly. At the foot of the giant Elevator Building, The Baltic Social was readying itself for its opening night. I went inside and was pleased to discover that the toilets had been wallpapered with the diaries of Vladimir Lenin. There was no call for Polari here – the barman spoke openly about his various encounters. I had a Black Russian at the bar and drew up a five-year plan.

I went on to visit about a dozen pubs and bars that evening, in the company of an Irishman and his Scouse fiancée, friends of friends who would become, by the ninth of that dozen, friends of my own. We finished at a place called Berry & Rye, a juke-joint style bar that has no official address. When Mick knocked on the door it was answered by one of Al Capone's grandchildren. 'Er, hi-yee,' said Mick, cool as you like. 'Can we, er, come in?' The grandchild of Al Capone lit a cigarette just so he could blow the smoke in Mick's face, before going on to politely inform us that there was currently a supper club in train, and to ask if we could possibly come back at eleven.

The next morning, I went to look at Antony Gormley's *Iron Men*, who stand in perpetual, tidal residence on Crosby Beach, a few miles north of the city centre. These men, who number a hundred, have a peculiar, corroding beauty, and their steadfast, ocean-facing postures reminded me of the city that hosts them. It is a brilliant experience seeing them ankle-deep in wet sand, stoic and inexplicable, the nature of their artwork changing ceaselessly as the tide drowns a score of them and the weather writes its review on their vulnerable forms. I applaud Gormley and whoever commissioned him, and I applaud Liverpool for refusing New York and hanging on to these brave men, who are a credit to the city, if not the world.

My next move was supposed to be in the direction of Port Sunlight on the Wirral Peninsula. As per Bryson, I was supposed to go and have a look at the model community there, established by William Lever for his soap workers at the end of the 19th century. But I couldn't bring myself to go. Why? Because I wanted these iron men – and their sombre, restless brilliance – to be the end of Liverpool, to be the city's souvenir, to be its last word. And so I skipped Port Sunlight and went to Wales instead.

20

Llandudno–Ludlow

I would have alighted at Chester had Josie Bryant answered my text message in time. As it was, I stayed put, bound for Llandudno, and was left to ponder what might have been. Josie has a four-year-old child in Chester, a very decent one by all accounts, though it's not hard to distinguish yourself at that age. Josie acquired this child a few years after graduating from university (the fruits of an English degree are a queer set), which is where I met her. It would be dishonest to suggest that we had been great friends at university; indeed I can't be sure if Josie counted me as a friend at all; but in any case I held a soft spot for this girl from Wrexham and would often distract myself with it during tiresome seminars on *Robinson Crusoe* or *The Merry Wives of Windsor*. And so it was with some disappointment, some small measure of sadness, that I passed Chester by, my inbox no heavier than it had been since proposing tea and dancing an hour before. It is only marginally hyperbolic to suggest that the fundamental direction and nature of one's life can depend on such things as a text message from Josie Bryant.

When I wasn't thinking about Josie and Chester and the capricious nature of life, I thought about the north Wales coast, and in particular the 'endless ranks of prison-camp caravan parks' identified by Bryson. For Bryson, the idea of staying at such a place for any period of time, and in a climate like Britain's, was a very odd one indeed. But the idea is less odd to the British. You can accuse the British of many things – politeness, stoicism, political correctness – but you cannot accuse them, at least since the end of the empire, of possessing a spirit of adventure.

Their holidays are a case in point. As a kid I used to holiday at a caravan park on the Isle of Wight every summer. If it was above thirteen degrees we would paddle in the sea. If it wasn't we would play the arcade machines and ride the go-carts for hours at a time. In the evening my dad would cook spaghetti bolognaise – we demanded it every night, without exception – and then my brother and I would wrestle and trade insults until it was time for bed.

An American may well scoff at such trifles, yet there is something deceptively attractive, and unexpectedly beneficent, about such simple holidays: the restrictions they impose can have, paradoxically, a liberating and unleashing – I might almost say humanising – effect. Faced with a tremendous lack of alternatives, the social focus on such holidays is inexorably shifted onto one another. Such a shift might at first upset some members of the holidaying party, but it rarely takes long before young Jack or Jill comes to see that a conversation with granddad or a period helping a sibling shell some peas can actually be quite rewarding undertakings. In short, such holidays are good for you, and if they have become less popular in Britain in recent years (which they indisputably have, notwithstanding the odd spike or flourish), then the British are poorer for the fact.

At Llandudno station the toilet facilities are locked at 14.20 each day, and I have a photograph to prove it. It was 14.35 when I arrived. I wasn't desperate or anything, just fancied going. I asked a man in the station's ticket office why the toilets were locked at 14.20 each day, but he was an old boy and didn't seem to understand what I was saying. I tried performing my enquiry, charades-style, but this only served to embarrass him. As far as introductions to a town go, this was not a glorious one.

I thought I'd have a coffee and a little something to eat at a place where the toilets weren't locked at 14.20, so I went into the first small restaurant I came to. But as soon as I entered the establishment, I sensed that I didn't want to order anything there, so suggested to the manageress, to explain my entrance, that I was lost, which I wasn't – I knew my hostel was just across the road on Charlton Street.

'What are you after?' she asked.

'The hostel.'

'No idea.'

'Okay never mind.'

'But Anne next door might know.'

Anne didn't know, but she had a suspicion, a strong one, that I needed to take the first right, which I didn't, I needed to take the first left. To maintain the façade of a person unsure of where he was going, which I generally maintain very well, I was therefore compelled to walk a hundred metres in the wrong direction before turning round. Was that British of me? To do something I didn't want or need to do in order not to appear rude?

I don't as a rule pay much heed to supposed national characteristics. When attempting to pin down a people – the British, the French, Librarians – the best we can hope for is to identify, by recourse to imperfect methodologies, imperfect patterns of behaviour, and then proceed (a hundred metres in the wrong direction) in the knowledge that for each example that conforms to the pattern, there will be several that don't.

At the hostel on Charlton Street, I was checked in by its two owners, one a kindly and soothing lady who quietly got on with the requisite paperwork, the other a younger man who finished all of his utterances, even the most inconsequential, with a short roar of laughter. As I unpacked in the dormitory, the younger man was good enough to acquaint me with the tea- and coffee-making facilities and then demonstrate how a bunk bed worked, waiting for a sign from me that I had understood perfectly what he was going on about before roaring with laughter and then moving on to the next thing he wanted to demystify, like the sink. We spoke a little about the town's attractions – the copper mine, Barnacles Fish and Chips, the station toilets – and then about the accommodation trade, the younger man explaining how the Grand Hotel, which sits at the foot of the Great Orme overlooking the bay, had been undercutting him with rates of £35 a night, bed, dinner and breakfast. I made a few noises that suggested sympathy, before making a mental note for next time.

I went to the Mostyn Art Gallery, established in the 1900s by the wife of one Lord Mostyn to exhibit the work of women artists. The current Lord Mostyn owns much of the town and much of London besides. I asked one of the gallery staff whether his Lordship cares for the artwork, which is of a subversive, anti-establishment bent. She said he comes in now and again, chortles a bit, tells everyone to keep up the good work and then sods off, no doubt to shoot something or procure a miniature train for one of his stately homes.

I enjoyed the gallery's exhibits very much, in particular Martha Rosler's iconoclastic alphabet of kitchen appliances, and Andrea Fraser's satirising of orthodox approaches to museum and gallery curatorship. It was all spunky and taut and intelligent. A shame that the locals, who are mostly over 80 years old, find so little value in this kind of work, or so I'm told. Might this gallery not serve a better purpose elsewhere, in Bangor or Aberystwyth, where there are younger populations? Or perhaps those with the most to learn or fear are the best audience for this brand of art?

After a walk along the promenade, which connects the town's famous headlands, Great and Little Orme, Bryson ate at a nondescript restaurant off Mostyn Street. There are about four-dozen restaurants that meet that description in Llandudno, so I was never going to find the one Bryson selected. Instead, I went to a seafood cafe that sits next to the terminus of the tram that runs up and down the Great Orme. I was alone in the cafe and so got talking with the waiter, a fashion and textiles graduate who now, armed with his degree certificate and ready to take on the world, dressed cod and haddock with dried parsley and lemon. He told me how he had spent the afternoon making a significant quantity of mushy peas, which is a longer and more complicated process than one might expect, and certainly not the sort of thing for someone without a university education.

Back in '94, Bryson stayed at one of the many Victorian hotels that line the promenade, selecting his on the promise of 'Colour TV and a Current Fire Certificate'. Not wanting to return to his hotel in a state of sobriety, Bryson went to a pub to get drunk and moan about the amount of bacteria in his lager. To do likewise, I went to the King's Head, opposite the cafe where I had dined. The pub was full of photographs of Llandudno in bygone years, one of which showed the town under construction back in the late 1860s. I asked the barman, or it might have been a fellow patron, how Llandudno had evolved, and I'm glad I did, because his account was long-winded and highly speculative, which is exactly the sort of social history I prefer.

Llandudno started in 1200, I was told, when a certain King Edward, either the first or third, gave some land to the Bishop of Bangor to play golf on. Then in about 1850, when the bishop's golf game fell to pieces and he tossed his clubs into the surf, an architect and surveyor from Liverpool put it to Lord Mostyn, who was the bishop's caddie and heir, that the marshy land between the town's north and south shores could be developed into a holiday resort – a proposal made plausible by the new railways.

Lord Mostyn liked the sound of this proposal but not, evidently, the sound of the architect's accent, for he soon fired the Scouser and employed one George Felton to oversee the resort's construction. Within a few weeks, or maybe months, but certainly not years, Llandudno's two-mile curving bay had a fetching promenade, a fetching sweep of Victorian hotels, and several fetching reviews on Trip Advisor. The Queen of Romania must have seen one of these reviews, because she took a five-week holiday here in 1890, considering the town a 'beautiful haven of peace'. This description was quickly translated into Welsh and made the town's motto, so that now one can't walk fifteen metres without encountering the phrase 'hardd, hafan, hedd', which reads less like a celebration of a town and more the complaint of someone who drank too much the night before.

I left the King's Head and went to The Palladium on Gloddaeth Street, a palatial 1920s building that used to be something wonderful and is now a Wetherspoon pub. I ate a chocolate sundae while reading the first chapter of Danielle Steele's *The Ring*, which I had found on a nearby shelf. As I read, a man walked by my table and kicked my ankle, telling me to sit up straight. We both laughed – he confidently, I nervously – but it actually hurt quite a bit. And that wasn't the final attack I would suffer that night. Later, as I paused outside a guesthouse to read the advertised amenities ('Portable Hairdryer', 'Stair Lift', 'Several Fire Escapes'), a passing teenager subjected me to a wolf whistle and called me treacle, perhaps because of my turquoise trousers, perhaps because I was still carrying the Danielle Steel novel.

Drawn by the sight of several dozen OAPs dancing and clapping, and keen to avoid any further altercations, I entered that guesthouse and ordered a pint. The atmosphere and carpet were far better than what I had found in The Palladium. A DJ – no younger than the guests – was playing songs from his laptop and doing a fine job of it. That said, I did question his choice of song to bring the night to a close. As the guests shuffled out into the hotel lobby and went looking for their rooms – and they took fresh pints with them, by the way – the DJ played Boyzone's 'If Tomorrow Never Comes', which struck me as a little close to the bone.

Llandudno is situated on a very narrow peninsula, which pokes out of the Welsh coast into the Irish Sea. As such it has two shorelines, with the town sandwiched between. I mention this now because as I walked from one shore to another in an effort to sober up, I discovered, about halfway between the two, a lifeboat station. That is to say, an *inland* lifeboat station. What, pray, is a lifeboat station doing inland? I put this question to the cashier at a nearby petrol station. The cashier, who was a local boy and a keen fisherman, explained how the people in charge of founding the lifeboat station had struggled with the predicament of having two shores to think about. Not wanting to appear to favour one side of the community or the other, it was decided that the station would be put between the two, amid residential streets, where nobody swims and nobody fishes, where, in short, there was precisely zero chance that it would be of use. As it stands, thanks to this act of well-meaning diplomacy, if you happen to start drowning during rush hour, you're pretty much destined to perish.

I went by bus the following morning to Blaenau Ffestiniog, which was once the second-biggest town in north Wales after Wrexham, and Oakeley Quarry the largest slate mine in the world. Then, of course, Time played its usual trick, and a combination of recession, the evacuation of the town's quarrymen to the trenches of France, and cheaper slate in Spain occasioned an inexorable downturn. Now the town relies on tourists, who come to see the slag heaps and use the EU-funded public toilets, whose decor pays homage to the town's lost industry.

The former attraction is worth a visit to Blaenau alone. Bryson suggested that the slag heaps 'gave the landscape an unearthly and eerie aspect like nothing else [he] had seen before in Britain'. And that is about right. The spread of grey-grim knolls are as startling an introduction to a place as Gormley's iron men at Crosby Beach. I would have been tempted, had I spoken Welsh, to ask the bus driver to turn around and descend once more.

The town's railway was closed in 1946 when the slate industry really started to falter. It has since been restored and reopened by enthusiasts, but to convey day-trippers rather than roof tiles. One of those day-trippers should have been Mr William Bryson, but owing to a timetabling peculiarity, Bryson contrived to miss his connecting steam service to Porthmadog by a few minutes. Faced with four hours to kill in a rainy backwater famous for what it *used to do*, Bryson naively attempts to chase away his gloomy mood, to eke out those four hours, with an omelette at the only open restaurant in town.

The restaurant's owners, sensing that Bryson was short of ideas, suggested a visit to the slate mine. Charitable as ever, Bryson met this proposal with one of his own: that such an excursion sounded about as appealing as a visit to the proctologist, which perhaps tells us more about Bryson than it does your average slate mine. With his mood now lower than ever, Bryson looked out the window at the greyest of prospects and consoled himself with the thought 'that one day this would be twenty years ago'. Well, Bill, that *was* twenty years ago, and that restaurant is no longer. The owners, rumour has it, threw in the towel not long after your visit, deciding that if yours was the face of modern tourism, then modern tourism could forget it.

Speeding away from Blaenau in a taxi, Bryson writes: 'I cannot tell you with what joy I beheld the sight of Blaenau disappearing into the distance behind me.' I beheld the same sight with no joy whatsoever. In fact, I beheld it sadly (and on board a steam train). It was perhaps this sadness, then, that made me react with such ambivalence to a young boy in his back garden, who, as the train and its single passenger choo-chooed past, waved at me like I was his own flesh and blood, as if waving at me were just about the finest thing he would ever get to do in his whole life. His face was practically on fire with joy, and yet all I wanted to do, perhaps to teach the boy at a young age that the world is a cruel, inexplicable place, was to put my middle finger up at the kid. How his face would have changed! How suddenly would his waving hand have frozen! As it was, I merely stared at the boy, wondering how a friendly man could have such unfriendly fantasies.

Bryson's first concern upon arriving in Porthmadog was to check in at the Royal Sportsman and then sit on the edge of his bed and eat Rich Tea biscuits and watch a Welsh soap opera called *Pobol Y Cwm*, wherein things like 'Wlch ylch aargh ybsy cwm dirty weekend' were said more or less constantly. But the biscuits and soap opera, I now see, were just a way of killing time before Bryson could do what he really wanted to, which was to visit the operational HQ of the Blaneau Ffestiniog Railway to register his sadness that, owing to some curious timetabling, he had been forced to while away four hours over a cheese omelette.

Bryson's sadness fell on deaf ears. According to his account, the employee with whom Bryson lodged his complaint was fussy, irrational, truculent and moustachioed. Moreover, he was all of these things to such a degree that Bryson was left with no option but to conclude that all train enthusiasts 'should be taken away and interned behind barbed wire'. I agree with Bryson, but with one caveat: that an exception is made for Michael Portillo, who, by appearing far too often on the BBC to demonstrate his enthusiasm for trains, does the United Kingdom a very fine public service, which is to make the rest of us appear better dressed by comparison.

Before heading back to the Sportsman, Bryson took a peek at the station's bookshop, where he found row upon row of salacious train videos promising '50 Minutes of Steam Action!', and an atmosphere not altogether dissimilar from that of a sex shop, prompting Bryson to wonder if 'there was an extra dimension to this train-spotting lark' that had never occurred to him before. Incidentally, this trip to the station bookshop is the last we hear from Bryson that evening. Are we to conclude that Bill was unable to resist the promise of 50 minutes of steam action, and so spent the bulk of his only evening in Porthmadog getting to grips with that film's artistic shortcomings?

Regardless of how Bryson spent his evening, I am confident he had more fun than me. After checking in at the Royal Sportsman, I asked at a convenience store what the town offered by way of evening diversions, and was told candidly that it was a toss-up between the 24-hour Tesco and the Chinese Takeaway. After a drink in the bar of the Sportsman, I went to a pub called The Station, hoping to run into a fussy, irrational, truculent and moustachioed man and buy him a pint. Instead I spoke for some time with an unfussy local arm wrestling champion, who told me about some youths who recently threw a pint of lager at a passing car. It was by no means an unpleasant conversation.

I got a take-away curry and returned with it to the hotel, which I really shouldn't have done, for the hotel manager had earlier made it clear that there was to be no take-away food in the rooms. But my non-conformist streak is a significant one, and so I overlooked the manager's rules and carefully entered the Sportsman and ascended its stairs with a chef's special between my legs.

There is little left to say about my only evening in Porthmadog, save that I ate the aforementioned curry in bed watching *Ffarme Ffactor* – like X-factor but for farmers – before doing a bit of research into *Pobol Y Cwm*, whose closest equivalent to Ken Barlow, I discovered, is Wyn Rees, who suffered a divorce and fractured pelvis on the same day – *on two occasions*.

Because the weather was horrid the next morning, no train services were running out of Porthmadog. Over breakfast I got speaking to a pair of Toyota executives who were in the area to visit a few showrooms. After learning of my predicament regarding the cancelled trains, one of the pair offered to drop me at the nearby town of Harlech, where I could pick up a train service to Shrewsbury.

Thus it was that I found myself riding shotgun in a Toyota GT860, while its tall owner graciously squeezed himself into one of the diminutive rear seats. I don't remember much of the 30-minute car ride as far as the local environment is concerned, but I do remember the nature of our conversation, which drifted off the topic of horsepower and the new Primus on just one occasion, when the driver accused his colleague of being an 'egg racist', on account of his not liking yolk. The accusation, not to mention the cramped conditions, didn't seem to bother the tall man, however. On the contrary: more than once did he allude to the pleasing 'novelty' of the situation he found himself in, as if novelty alone were enough to make any situation pleasant, like being squashed into the back of a car and called an egg racist, for example. And perhaps it is so. Perhaps novelty can alter our experience of a situation or a place or a person in such a way. I am no psychologist, but I wouldn't be surprised to learn of studies that demonstrate how a person tied to an affluent routine is more prone to melancholy and boredom than a person who wilfully moves between states of relative austerity.

The small town of Harlech was largely still in bed when we arrived. I knocked on the window of the Blue Lion cafe, wherein a lady was baking scones and setting up for the day. She gestured that the cafe wouldn't be open for another half an hour. I gestured that it would be a very nice thing in any case if I could just sit inside until opening time, on account of it being frigid out here and toasty in there.

After performing a quick risk assessment through the window, the lady let me in and sat me down in a warm corner. A couple of minutes later, and without my bidding, she brought me a coffee and a scone. Her name was Annette. Halfway through my scone two more staff members arrived, and the three women settled down to a session of gossip. The gossip had the quality of renewable energy, and each of the women was a master spinner of the stuff – dexterous, fanciful, indefatigable – and I was reminded of the old clay throwers of Stoke-on-Trent, who were able to conjure the most fabulous things from a damp lump of slip. It was as if gossiping was the job of these women and they were getting paid by the piece. So productive were they that I struggled to keep up with the various storylines and subtexts.

Much of their talk concerned Annette's son, who works on the oil rigs and is rumoured to be in want of a wife. From what I could tell, there wasn't a woman in town that Annette hadn't interviewed for the role. One of the women who hadn't proved suitable – a yoga teacher in her forties called Louise – was suggested to be my type. Annette said that Louise didn't have much of a social life and would almost certainly be free that afternoon. Not wanting to seem ungrateful, I suggested that ordinarily I would have been interested in getting to know Louise, but that I had to get to Blackpool via Ludlow by midnight, and wasn't ever planning to come back. The women shook their heads in unison, as if my going to Blackpool via

Ludlow and never coming back were somehow a dereliction of duty.

Waiting on the platform for the 9.04 to Shrewsbury, I remembered what had happened to Bryson on the equivalent morning, and on the equivalent platform, twenty years before. Waiting for his train, Bryson managed to anger a man on his way to work by standing in that man's preferred square-metre of platform. Despite his obvious distress, however, the man was unable or unwilling to communicate it. He left Bryson well alone. Bryson takes the man's behaviour as evidence that the British – and not this man in particular – are damagingly incapable of expressing how they feel. To further support his hypothesis, Bryson then recalls a young man who was once lavishly sick on a train to Cardiff. After vomiting, Bryson recounts, the young man quickly alighted the train and ran off into the night. For Bill, the salient aspect of this story is less the fact that the man was lavishly sick and more the fact that despite being decorated with chunks of vomit the surrounding passengers behaved – 'in that most extraordinary British way' – as if nothing had happened. Is that a British way? Are the British so routinely and reliably spineless, so uncomplaining, so willing to keep calm and carry on? I for one wouldn't have thought twice before running after the lavishly sick man and then (while catching my breath) setting things straight: 'I'm terribly sorry sir – and I hope you – don't mind me – er – pointing this out – but I think you – I think you – I'm terribly sorry but I think you forgot your newspaper.'

At Shrewsbury I learnt that my onward train to Ludlow was subject to an hour's delay. I left the station and went for walk, pausing first at the local library, which is housed in a 16th-century former grammar school. One of the school's pupils was Charles Darwin, author of the Booker Prize-winning epic *On the Origin of Species* (which is just a tad long, in my opinion, and too derivative to suggest genius). I know that Darwin was a pupil at the school because a statue of him looking bored and hungry sits in front of the building. In a nod to Darwin's evolutionary bent, some local smart alec had placed a bunch of bananas in his lap, the cheeky monkey.

For the short time I was there, Shrewsbury had me in a spell. All of its favourable features – the station, the library, its pitched, gently bending high street – were made more so by their being a surprise to me. Shrewsbury was made better by my innocence. Were we able to remain innocent and unknowing throughout our lives, would our experience of the world be improved, I wonder? I should say that it would, for we would once more be as children, constantly taken aback, constantly impressed, forever enamoured and provoked. For the innocent, the whole world is a novelty, and novelty, as we have seen with the Toyota executive, can render even the most uncomfortable experiences enjoyable.

But innocence is not easily held on to. From the first minutes of our lives we slowly surrender it. In its place come knowledge, prejudice, familiarity, boredom, indifference, complacency and expectation. To a large degree the trading of innocence for experience is to our advantage: one wouldn't last long as an adult if one remained as guileless and excitable as a toddler. (How many toddlers do you know that can hold down a job, for example?) Nonetheless, I wouldn't mind having a bit more toddler in me. For on those rare occasions when I feel innocent once more – as in Shrewsbury for that long, full half-hour – it is a very fine thing.

And so to Ludlow, of which I was not innocent, having read several times Bryson's assessment of the place, which was altogether favourable. It is not my habit to do so, but allow me to present a short profile of Ludlow, a résumé if you will, based on what I learned of an evening there.

Ludlow is a Shropshire market town of about 11,000 people; it was founded by the Normans to keep an eye on the Welsh, who were known troublemakers; it was built to a grid pattern, which I failed to notice; it is at the confluence of two rivers and atop a small hill; it has a castle and a highly regarded parish church, which has a decent set of misericords, whatever the hell they are; and the town is said to have been built on the backs of sheep, for it was the wool industry that underpinned the local economy at the time of the church's construction. As far as résumés go, it is not a bad one. More often than not, Ludlow would get the job.

It was to the church that I went first, not because I'm pious, but simply because I wanted to pause in a quiet place for a while – I had been on the move for most of the day, and ached for a short respite. I didn't get it, however, as the church has one of the most exacting and voracious volunteers in Europe. In an accent that made the Queen sound like an apprentice joiner, and within a minute of my entering, I was told by this volunteer that I would struggle to produce anything half as good as Bryson so long as I lived, that the church has a 91 per cent average on Trip Advisor, and that the misericords are a fine set indeed.

Like most people who are blatantly smarter than me, I found this lady at once splendid and unbearable. Because her friendliness was loaded with the quality of enmity, she brought to mind Nietzsche's conception of a best friend. By pointing out our limitations and misdeeds, such friend-enemies, according to Nietzsche, drag us painfully closer to self-understanding, and thereby do us a favour. We are made better by the bruises they inflict. It is good for me – so the theory goes – to know that I am destined to fall short of Bryson.

There is a pleasing sense of disorder in Ludlow. Despite, as noted, the town being arranged according to a grid pattern, its streets and side streets seem to appear from nowhere, lending any brief exploration of the town a measure of unpredictability. Furthermore, Ludlow's relative architectural uniformity (the town is awfully well conserved) makes navigation more challenging. That isn't to say that Ludlow doesn't have striking individual buildings (the Feathers Hotel and the Buttercross are examples), only that one can't rely on a particularly gruesome multi-storey car park or a sudden concrete overpass to regain their bearings. National chains – Greggs, Nandos, Tesco – have a small presence in the town, making it yet harder to lay down obvious, corporate co-ordinates. Ludlow's ability to discombobulate is, of course, for the better. The element of surprise improves the urban experience.

I went to see the Ludlow and District Cats Protection League on Old Street. Bryson had been intrigued by the fussiness of the organisation's boundaries, and had wondered what would happen if he was spotted disappointing a cat a few yards beyond them. This thought led Bryson to consider the welfare of British animals in general, citing the fact that the British passed a law to protect animals 60 years before they passed a law to protect children. As with the angry man on the platform, Bill extrapolates from this isolated example a general truth – namely, that the British dote on their pets but can't stand their kids – before suggesting that there is nothing that makes him 'feel more like an outsider in Britain than the nation's attitude toward animals'.

I know that I'm starting to get on Bill's back a bit regarding his habit of finding rules in examples, but is it at all viable that a nation-state as complicated, variegated and unsteady as Britain can have an appreciable *attitude* toward something? Britain can no more have an attitude than it can have a preference – for yellow, say, or Nicole Kidman. I've already mentioned that I place little stock in such broad-stroke characterisations, on account of their being more-or-less erroneous. But the fact remains that they make for amusing observations and anecdotes, and even if they bear little truth, little social value, the people to whom the observations pertain – in this case the British – can often find much amusement and consolation in them.

It must be so, otherwise *Notes from a Small Island*, with its flippant, tongue-in-cheek attempts to put its finger on the British, wouldn't have been voted Britain's favourite book about the British. Maybe the book is so loved because it is plainly untrue; because it is plainly a fiction; because it is plainly an overly generous and confident and optimistic caricature of the British and their ways. A more honest account of Britain would necessarily be more indecisive, complicated, doubtful and inconclusive, and therefore less endearing, less palatable, less readable. No one wants 300 pages of level-headed circumspection, no matter its veracity. Bryson's is a fine book, but it does not, by any stretch of the imagination, capture the British. For the British – and they ought to be proud of the fact, whoever the hell they are – are not ready to be caught.

21

Blackpool–Morecambe

I was met at Blackpool North station by David, a professional Santa and single father of two, and my host for the night. Despite it being early December and nearly midnight, David was sporting a Hawaiian shirt and sunglasses, and a look that suggested that once he started talking he wouldn't stop for 24 hours.

I was tired, ever so tired, and not at all sure whether I had the necessary patience and open heart to benefit from David's company, to endure what promised to be a colourful, slightly crazed brand of hospitality. I had made an online application to stay on David's couch for the very reasons that now made me hesitant. I had wanted to meet a character, an eccentric, a proper Blackpudlian. But that was then. Now I just wanted to be alone and unconscious. 'Welcome to sunny Blackpool!' said David, taking me into his arms like a lost elf. 'You're one of 10 million who will visit this year. It used to be 17 million before Benidorm happened.'

David's flat looked how a flat might if a couple of seven year olds were forced to cohabit without supervision – toys in the microwave; mud, sand and pebbles in the bath and sink; juvenile aphorisms scribbled on the wall with crayon ('bedtime is evil', 'sisters are crap'). Taking a seat on the floor between two Cabbage Patch dolls, I asked my host if Blackpool's famous illuminations had evolved much over the last twenty years; if

Bryson had been right to call them tacky and inadequate. As if channelling the subject matter, David's face reddened. 'They didn't need to evolve,' he said peremptorily. 'They have always been spectacular.'

David made some tea, rounded up some blankets and put on *Les Misérables*. I used to have a very narrow-minded, splenetic opinion of musicals, believing them to be a lower art form, to be inherently frivolous. It seemed self-evident to me that anything containing so much singing and dancing couldn't possibly be serious or meaningful or instructive. There's no singing in Joyce, I would argue, or Hitchcock, or Fellini, or Caravaggio. The very popularity of musicals, I would go on, was further evidence of their simplicity. The mob was stupid I would say, the mob went to Blackpool for their holidays, the mob watched soap operas and musicals and read Dan Brown and Danielle Steel.

Then, when I was about 24, I saw *West Side Story* and got hooked on *Gavin and Stacey* and came to see how fatuous it was to think that popularity was in anyway an indicator of inferiority. Needless to say, and to cut to the chase, I enjoyed *Les Misérables* very much, particularly the bit when Anne Hathaway sings about how disappointing prostitution is.

I woke the next morning surrounded by Rapunzel and Pocahontas – not altogether unpleasant. David was keen to show me around town. After a breakfast of tea and frozen pizza, we went directly to Blackpool's iconic tower, put up in 1894 and modelled on the one in Paris. We climbed 500 feet to the viewing gallery, which was empty. I know it was early on a weekday and out of season, but still, can you imagine the Eiffel Tower, even on a solemn winter morning, having anything less than a few hundred people either waiting to go up it, going up it, or up it? Granted, Blackpool is not Paris, but their respective towers are of a kind – striking, handsome, thrilling to climb, exemplars of show-off engineering – and no matter the season or the time of the day it was a pity that David and I were alone at the tower's top, alone in looking down upon the town, alone in our mutual appreciation for all that sat and spun and shifted beneath us.

As a father pointing out the constellations, David indicated the sites below: the police station on Bonny Street where he once spent a night after an altercation with his ex-wife; the recently laid Comedy Carpet, an acre of gags and sketches etched into the promenade; the silver hangars of the old airport at Stanley Park, now so many elephant enclosures housing so many Dumbos, each waiting, as Blackpool, to take off once more; the Grand Theatre, where *Peter Pan* was opening that night with someone from *Hollyoaks* or *Emmerdale* or *Pobol y Cwm* in the leading role; the Winter Gardens, Bloomfield Road, the three piers, a litter of high-rise blocks to the east – it was all there, cowering silently in the rain below.

David went for a job interview at Morrisons. Having nothing better to do, I threw stones into the Irish Sea, tried to make a rough castle from damp sand, and thought briefly of turning my trousers up and walking towards Belfast. But then I remembered the water's cleanliness and thought better of it. It had been dirty enough back in 1994 for the local council to disown it, to officially take it off the map so that if anybody went for a swim and came out with extra fingers and polio the local council could shrug and say, 'We told you it wasn't a beach.' On a bench a few metres away, a woman with thirteen fingers and polio was sitting eating a platter of chips and an ice cream. She wore a look of quiet determination, as if working through a particularly tall pile of ironing. I asked her about the sea, whether it was clean. 'If you go in,' she said, 'you're right to take bog roll with yer.'

I played bingo on Rigby Road. It was 30p a game and everybody playing was entitled to free tea and coffee. I received a swift tutorial from a caller on his break. Of course I knew how bingo worked. I simply wanted to hear this young man's explanation, to see how he dealt with me, to note his manner, mark his words, watch his expressions. I was impressed: he was courteous and lucid and had a good sense of humour, even attempting a skilful pun to do with balls dropping. I played one game without success and then watched the others for a while. It seemed incredibly easy to win. One woman even managed to win a travel iron despite being asleep.

Near Bank Hey Street there is a Methodist church that has conceded its ground floor to Shoe Zone. Worshippers, one presumes, must now enter the church via a fire exit. Corporation Street looked lonely and out of luck. I asked the proprietor of a hardware store whether Blackpool was finally starting to come to a halt, to lose whatever remained of its centuries-old appeal.

He told me that he first came to Blackpool as a boy, during one of the famous Wakes Weeks, when the mills and factories of Lancashire and Yorkshire would close for seven days to carry out maintenance, forcing their entire workforces to take a week's holiday en masse. Working towns twice the size of Blackpool – Warrington, Bradford, Barnsley, Preston – would descend on the resort for a week at a time. Then, from the 1950s onwards, the workplaces of Lancashire and Yorkshire – of industrial Britain – stopped closing for a week to carry out maintenance and started closing full stop. The number of people visiting Blackpool has fallen steadily since, but not to a fatal or catastrophic degree. Ten million still visit each year, more than any other resort in the UK. 'What do they come for?' I asked. He shrugged. 'What did you come for?' he asked.

Every hotel or guesthouse along its south shore boasts of being Blackpool's best. One such offered a five-course-meal for £10. I was tempted to drop in despite not being hungry, because I wanted to know which five courses a hotel could possibly offer a person, bearing in mind all the miscellaneous overheads involved when serving a meal in a hotel restaurant, for a mere £10. In defiance of the foul weather, I spent a good few minutes outside that hotel scrutinising its menu. And I'm glad I did, for it materialised – and I wouldn't have enjoyed this coming as a surprise – that the steamed vegetables that came alongside the roast pork and potatoes constituted a course on their own. I have a high threshold for egregiously misleading advertising, but this hotel, with its five courses for £10, was unequivocally taking the pineapple.

Blackpool has a new batch of trams. Why do I mention the fact? Are these trams particularly elegant? Particularly fast? Particularly anything? Well, no. I mention them because I feel I ought to. After all, one of the principal objectives of this project was to mark how Britain had changed over the previous two decades. But I must confess that this objective has slipped further and further from the forefront of my mind as the journey has gone on. Not because – or, rather, not entirely because – I feel that such comparisons (closed! open! restored! ruined!) lack value. No, the reason that this comparative objective has grown steadily less important and less instinctive is that *Notes from a Small Island* does not offer much to compare *against*. The book is not the work of a social historian, nor a geographer, nor a political commentator, nor a cartographer, nor an architect, nor an urban theorist. It is anecdotal, flippant and playful. It is an impression of Britain rather than a thoroughgoing portrait in the realist mode. Which is for the better, I feel. Imagine that Britain were a house and that Bryson had produced a detailed inventory – floorboards, scuffed; bulbs, dim; garden, overgrown – and that I had undertaken to produce a diligent, contemporary equivalent. Maybe the result would have been useful, in a socio-cultural sense, but it also would have been very dull. I mean, how many inventories trend on social media? So yeah, Blackpool has a new batch of trams, and the illuminations haven't evolved because they haven't needed to, and the congregation of the Methodist church on Bank Hey Street now get 20 per cent off at Shoe Zone. Do with this information what you will.

The famous Pleasure Beach amusement park was obviously hibernating, but its gates were open so I entered and wandered about as an archaeologist might a group of ruins, marvelling at the quiet good looks of the old-fashioned, unadorned, unlit fairground rides. Hard to believe it, but the Pleasure Beach was once the second-most-popular attraction in Europe behind the Vatican. Imagine if the Pope had decided to visit the Pleasure Beach. Google Maps would surely have crashed, unable to cope with the sudden surge of day-trippers burning a hole in the side of Lancashire.

Outside the park is yet another expensive public art piece – the world's largest disco ball. Although diverting, such sculptures and installations can seem like consolation prizes for lost industries, so that the experience of them is somehow tainted with a sense of loss or misfortune. I'm not saying that such things shouldn't be there. Nor am I saying that Britain's erstwhile mines and mills and docks should be reopened; it is for a smarter person than I to decide the course of post-industrial Britain. I am merely saying that one's experience of these artworks, the harsh fruit of industrial demise, is bittersweet.

I bought some dinner at a Co-op, managing to thoroughly scrutinise the discounted goods section without appearing to do so. I ate my reduced pork pies on Birley Street, upon whose length giant metallic ribbons have been planted to form an unusual archway, with each ribbon containing a sound system and wearing a dozen oversize light bulbs in various shades, turning the street into a perpetual disco.

At the bottom of Birley Street is the Rose and Crown, where I ordered a pint of lager and watched as England were drawn in a World Cup group with Italy, Uruguay and Costa Rica, which I fancy they'll have little problem progressing from. I took my pint outside and watched, one by one, the street's bulbs come on, and then several children dancing to the Pet Shop Boys as their father waited in line at the chip shop.

Watching those children and hearing that music, I was inexplicably happy. The man from the hardware store walked past and I called after him and he seemed pleased to see me and we joked about the music and the fancy street lights and how Blackpool likes to waste money on such things. Seeing the man contributed to my happiness. The chance encounter, the brief sensation of knowing people in this town, was enough for me. And so I moved on.

The old train station in Morecambe is now a nightclub. The Winter Gardens, which once hosted the cream of British entertainers, now calls for volunteers to man its box office. The local newspapers warn of missing cats and more delays on the M62. Victoria and Queen Streets – two of Morecambe's most crucial – are routinely deserted, even on Saturday afternoons. As Blackpool, Morecambe has slipped a few notches. Whereas Blackpool can save face behind its mighty frame, Morecambe has no such defence. The town has the quality of a frail pensioner, once virile and bolshie, once proud as punch, once an exuberant hostess, now too weary to leave the house.

It wasn't always like this of course. Morecambe once took as many visitors as Blackpool and boasted some of the best amusements in Europe. Bryson takes pains to illustrate just how great Morecambe had once been – 'eight music halls, eight cinemas, an aquarium, a funfair, a menagerie, a revolving tower, a boating garden, a Summer Pavilion, the largest swimming pool in Britain, two piers' – and just how far it has fallen. That isn't to say that Morecambe has lost all its charms. Its bay, according to Bill, is 'easily one of the most beautiful in the world, with unforgettable views across to the green and blue Lakeland hills'. Well, the view can't be that unforgettable because I've forgotten it. Perhaps I was distracted by other things. An establishment called Northern Relics, perhaps, which I mistook for a tourist information point.

Enoch Powell gave a speech in Morecambe in 1968. I wasn't there to hear it – my mother was seven years old at the time – but read about it as a student. Powell, you'll remember from Chapter 17, was the Conservative politician who gave the 'rivers of blood speech', which warned of the perils of an ethnically diverse population. His Morecambe speech came from the same school of thought. In what has come to be known as the 'Morecambe Budget', Powell outlined how the next Tory government would rescue the nation from financial ruin by slashing tax rates, privatising national assets and cancelling all grants and subsidies. Should the Conservatives retain power at the 2015 general election, it wouldn't surprise me if, in order to demonstrate the party's commitment to sustainability, David Cameron or George Osborne or Boris Johnson were to take a trip to Morecambe to recycle Powell's address. I can imagine the press release. 'The Sustainable Conservative Party: Recycling Old Policies.'

Bryson spent his afternoon in Morecambe strolling around imagining the town in its heyday. One of the things Morecambe did in its heyday, and that I was happy to spend some time imagining, was to hold the Miss Great Britain beauty contest each year. I happened to meet Miss Great Britain 1985 when I attended a conference at the University of Lancaster in 2011. She was presenting a paper on the role of poetry in the fall of the Ottoman Empire. We went for drinks after the conference, which was when she mentioned her Morecambe success. I didn't believe her at first, frankly, and got to thinking that beauty contests aren't the meritocracies we suppose them to be. Perhaps it's about who you know.

As well as imagining Morecambe in its heyday, Bryson spent time reflecting on those attempts made by the town to compete with Blackpool, including the ill-fated Mr Blobby amusement park, which closed within thirteen weeks of opening, and just a matter of days after Bryson's visit. (God knows how, but I like to think the two were related.)

For Bryson such attempts to keep up with Blackpool were misguided, not least because Morecambe's 'charm, and certainly its hope, lies in being *not* Blackpool'. This is a nice sentiment, but not the most effective of consolations. Imagine a pair of twins who until their mid-twenties were equally excellent at school and university, equally lauded at work, equally successful on Tinder. Then one of the pair began to suffer setback after setback, while their sibling continued as they were. Would it console the fallen twin if they were told that their demise was charming, that their demise made them special, that their demise was their only hope? It wouldn't wash, would it? No, Morecambe's only hope isn't that it's *not* Blackpool. Morecambe's only hope is that Blackpool is bombed by North Korea.

At Rita's Cafe on Marine Parade I ate a plate of chips, cheese and gravy and drank a cup of tea. The cafe was full of locals of several generations, wearing Manchester United and

Morecambe football shirts, talking keenly and animatedly as they waited on their Roast Chicken Dinner for £3.70, or their chicken curry and chips for £2.10. Morecambe might have lost its pools and piers and Mr Blobby parks, but at least there are still folk here, eating and chatting and winding each other up, courting and bickering and making the most of it.

I asked Rita if Morecambe were playing at home that day. Despite being in the middle of doing something – filling a baguette, if I remember – she volunteered to google it for me. Yes, Morecambe were at home. I asked Rita how to get to the stadium. Again she googled. I would need to take the 6A bus from outside the cafe, departing at 14.25. I asked if I could leave my backpack with her and then collect it after the match. No need to google that: of course I could. So obliging was she, I thought about asking Rita if she wouldn't mind writing up my notes on Blackpool, and emailing my grandparents, and making a start on my Christmas shopping.

A rather down-at-heel looking gentleman had set up a makeshift betting station outside the stadium. I put £5 on Morecambe to win 4-0, despite the team not having won at home for six months, then found a spot behind the goal with the home supporters. The remaining three sides of the ground were sparsely populated. In fact, there was not a single person in the away end. Not one Cheltenham fan had considered a trip to Morecambe to watch two-dozen metrosexuals run around a field worth the effort and expense involved.

There are plenty of things that I could write about the Morecambe versus Cheltenham match, but I won't. I won't because if you want to read a beautiful, mindful account of a travelling writer at a provincial, lower-league football match then you should take Priestley's *English Journey* and turn to page 138, and there rejoice in the writer's gentle, even-handed discussion of why crowds of men will 'pay shillings they can barely afford to see twenty-two professionals kick a ball about'.

What I will say is that for the second half of the match I relocated to the other end of the ground, where I stood alone upon the terrace as a pretend Cheltenham fan, a sight that drew ironic cheers from the home fans, my erstwhile comrades, who couldn't be sure if I was a turncoat or a prankster or a genuine Cheltenham supporter who had gotten delayed on the M6. Morecambe did not win 4–0, for the record. My bet came to nothing, but I'm glad I laid it all the same.

22

Lake District

Bryson stayed for a couple of nights at the Old England Hotel in Bowness, which used to be privately owned but is now in the hands of the McDonald's chain, and is one of several of Bryson's old haunts to have since been gobbled up by large parent companies. I went through to the hotel's dining room, where Bryson spent his first morning in the Lakes thinking about the weather. He was prompted to do so by a report in *The Times* about a 'blizzard' in East Anglia. Bryson gives this report short shrift, dismissing the 'blizzard' as nothing but a breeze with drizzle, and the reporter as nothing but a hyperbolic sissy who ought to be taken off the news desk and redeployed in the staff canteen. If there's anything striking about the English weather, Bill muses, it's that 'there isn't very much of it'.

And this is just fine by Bill, who appreciates being able to 'wear the same type of clothing every day of the year'. And he is not joking. By recourse to YouTube, I discovered that the jacket Bill's wearing on the jacket of *Notes from a Small Island* is the very same jacket as the jacket he was wearing at a book reading in Lewes in 1996, a book reading in Ayrshire in 1999, and a press junket in Slough in 2002. I very much sympathise with Bryson's aversion to shopping, but wearing the same jacket for the bulk of your adulthood is potentially a bit much. Maybe the guy should move somewhere with a more diverse climate – Outer Mongolia, perhaps – just so he can get some new clothes.

After sitting around in the dining room for several hours thinking about the weather, Bryson considers it time he did some exercise, and so takes a walk through to the residents' lounge, where he orders a tuna sandwich and a caramel latte. (Yes, another tuna sandwich. I declined this one. There is no inspiring adage that instructs to try everything twice.) Mid-sandwich, Bryson is confronted by a pompous English couple, who accuse him of being an American and serving obscene portions and corrupting the Queen's English and being too friendly. On the latter point – over friendliness – the pompous woman observes that you've 'only to chat to a stranger for five minutes [in America] and they think you've become *friends*'.

Needless to say, Bryson doesn't enjoy the encounter ever so much, in particular the accusation that Americans have been buggering the English language, and so he leans across to remind the couple that 'whether they appreciate it or not British speech has been enlivened beyond measure by words created in America, words that they could not do without, and that one of these words was moron' – before neglecting to mention that another was fanny pack, and that another was ridiculosity. Bryson then exits the lounge in as unfriendly a fashion as he can manage, but not before encouraging the couple to become his friend on Facebook and scribbling a note of complaint for hotel management vis-à-vis the tuna sandwich, which really ought to have been a triple-decker and served with fries.

Because the Old England is now owned by a distant parent company, there wasn't a member of staff within a 400-mile radius permitted to make a decision on significant issues, namely my heartfelt application to stay at the hotel at little to no cost, and so the matter was kicked into the long grass, to be dealt with three weeks hence by Ronald at McDonald's HQ.

But I won't whinge too much, for I soon found some excellent accommodation a few miles north at the Merewood Hotel, a detached Georgian country house set in twenty acres on the right hip of Lake Windermere. Unusually – unprecedentedly in fact – the hotel manager listened to my sales pitch with an almost wild degree of enthusiasm. As I rambled on, she continued to nod encouragingly and make sympathetic noises that suggested that I was on the right track, that I was saying the right things, that all this was very good news indeed. She was like a fawning undergraduate listening to her favourite professor. After I'd finished my spiel she took a step back, put her hands on her hips, and then took a few deep breaths, simply blown away by it all.

'Well, Ben, I have absolutely never heard of this Bill Bryson you speak of, and nor do I have an especial interest in literature, but that is all by the by, because everything you just said sounds *lovely*.' I told her how refreshing it was to find a hotelier with a heart, with a sense of civic responsibility, supportive of the Big Society, what with all those imported drones down at the Old England. 'Yes!' she cried. 'Yes they *are*, aren't they? Ha! Well, Ben, we shall show *them*.'

We showed them first of all by my having a long bubbly bath. That done, I adorned a fluffy dressing gown, settled onto the bed, told the hotel manager that it probably wasn't a good idea to open another bottle and that she really ought to get back to work, and then acquainted myself with the work of

Beatrix Potter, famous around these parts for her Peter Rabbit children's books.

Bryson isn't a fan of said books, considering them somewhat 'soppy'. I found them anything but. In *The Tale of the Greedy Fox*, for example, Peter and Lily and Benjamin (all rabbits) try to pilfer a cucumber from the allotment of a fox called Mr Toad. They are caught in the act and Mr Toad rightly gives the trio a rollicking, but perhaps goes too far when he demands to know why on earth they would want to eat cucumber when they could eat, 'oh I don't know, RABBIT STEW!', which struck me as a bit close to the bone, and a somewhat premature introduction of the concept of cannibalism to an audience of mostly under-8s.

In any case, it seems to me that Potter's stories aren't as 'soppy' as Bryson will have us believe. If this sort of stuff is soppy for Bryson, I dread to think what he considers 'hard' or 'dark' or 'twisted'. Perhaps Bryson's tolerance for this sort of literature is a product of an American upbringing, which cannot fail to influence an individual's sense of the macabre and the dramatic. In Britain, after all, political melodrama is a sudden change of upholstery in the House of Lords, while in the States, bodybuilders are elected and incumbents get erotically relieved while on the phone to Iran. In Britain, criminals go to self-help seminars; in the States, they're electrocuted. In Britain, people go to the funfair to *calm down*; in the States, you go to vomit and snap neck ligaments.

The upshot of all this is that when a Brit finally does go abroad, they are likely to find everything thrilling beyond belief, whereas when an American goes abroad they are likely to find everything somewhat underwhelming. In short, if one is exposed to an American way of doing things for long enough, one's understanding of such things as scale and horror and value-for-money will be ineluctably altered, so that when one learns of a blizzard in East Anglia, or comes across a quietly barbaric children's story, one is liable to dismiss such items as mere trifles.

After his restful stay at the Old England, Bill attempts something altogether more taxing – to reach the 'fabled summit of Bow Fell', the sixth-highest of the Lakeland hills. He is collected from his hotel by a couple of mates – John Price and David Partridge, who sound made up, to be honest – and then taken to another near Bassenthwaite, where the three men ready themselves for the task ahead, which is to say they tuck their socks into their trousers and apply sun cream to each other's fundamental protrusions.

They needn't have bothered with the sun cream, however, for as the trio made their ascent the weather steadily worsened. Before long a combination of 'truly menacing' fog, jagged sleet and ferocious gusts of wind had conspired to make the going all but impossible (and here's me thinking that Britain had no weather). At one point the conditions got so bad that Bryson seriously contemplated taking off his jacket – the jacket from the book jacket – and replacing it with something less suggestive of an elderly landowner and more suggestive of a fell walker in winter. At the end of their odyssey, the three men celebrated reaching the summit by untucking their trousers and eating several cheese and pickle sandwiches. I would sincerely love to meet these guys.

I didn't climb Bow Fell. I wanted to, but was warned against it on several occasions, most persuasively in the bar of the Merewood Hotel on the afternoon of my arrival.

'You got a compass?'

'No.'

'Map?'

'No.'

'Trousers that tuck into socks?'

'Er ...'

'Life insurance?'

'No.'

'You do know people lose limbs climbing Bow Fell?'

'No.'

'You do know people get lost altogether?'

'No.'

'You do know about the successful American who fell off the top after too many cheese and pickle sandwiches?'

And so it was that I set off from the Merewood that afternoon with the modest ambition of climbing a hill a lot smaller than Bow Fell. But I didn't know which one. In Ambleside – a small lakeside town about fifteen minutes' walk from the hotel – I entered a bookshop and asked which hills were suitable for a man of my physique and in this weather. At first the shop keeper thought he'd have a bit of fun by suggesting that perhaps I should see how I got on walking to the One-Stop and back. Then he pointed out the window and said: 'Climb Wansfell. It's over there.'

Climbing Wansfell, I would stop every 50 yards to collect my breath and take in the accumulating view, each instalment of which gave at once more and less: the rivers were slighter in their running, the valleys sharper in their falling, the cars and buses more discreet in their passing, the sheep softer in their bleating, the shop doors of Ambleside more silent in their opening and closing. Each 50 yards gave not only a new visual perspective but also a new emotional one, the dales and fells and sheep and shops somehow gaining nobility and gravitas in their slow recession. Each 50 yards gave a new dose of acid to my muscles, and with it a better understanding of why people did this, and why Wordsworth in particular did this, why he withstood the mocking and heckling of London's fashionable intelligentsia and continued to write poems about hills and daffodils and how humbled and renewed and better they made him feel, how humbled and renewed and better they made *him*.

At the top, legs weak, chest tight, sweatshirt wet, I gave a long fond sigh of celebration, cried out silently at the thickness of life, took off the wet sweatshirt, and the wet T-shirt, and threw my hair around like someone in a shampoo ad. I looked down on the land – the view was good; you'd be irked if it wasn't – and tried to think of all the things that had been taken from it. The lead and copper and graphite and slate, pulled from tops and bottoms and sides and seams, like so many appendices, so much offal. The pencils and axes and tiles and coins, each withdrawn in early forms, ready to be embossed and laid and sharpened, ready to wreak havoc, slay trees, make prose and verse. And wool. Wool pulled from the hillside, from sheep-side, so many pullovers.

On the other side of the summit there was a wind trap and a rare, notable silence that was beautiful, that I wanted to photograph. The eastward land threw up loose, imperfect associations: *Macbeth*, *Wuthering Heights*, Dartmoor. The long drystone walls, like great Chinese miniatures, drew lines in the wilderness. A fell runner with the whitest legs and shortest shorts (think uncooked turkey drumsticks) approached from afar at a rate of one or two millimetres a minute, his heavy breathing a clear threat to my silence. Ten minutes later he passed and said nothing, just winked at me as he went, a coy encouragement to do more with my life.

The eastward track led me to Troutbeck and offered an easy descent. It was nice to walk with my hands in my pockets, to think about upcoming birthdays or lapsed relations, to hum a tune rather than pant and groan, to spot a cat in the distance, a black fish out of water. At a pub called the Mortal Man, I drank a pint of Sally Birkett's Ale in the garden beneath enclosing almond hills, each crowned with a run of stubborn mist. I wanted to phone my mother in that garden, and if not my mother then my father, and if not my father then my grandmother, someone that I loved in any case, but there was no signal and so I couldn't, and the desire had to suffice.

23

Newcastle–Durham–Ashington

I was hoping the train from Carlisle to Newcastle would go through the Pennines as I had done – beautifully, thrillingly – in my campervan a few years before. But instead it went around them – sensibly, boringly – and as a result the scenery, when compared to the Lake District, seemed unfinished. It is a pity for anything to suffer by comparison, I thought, recalling the unhelpful precedent set by my ex-girlfriend's ex-boyfriend, who was a porn star.

I am tempted to present Newcastle as it happened, as I recorded it in raw form, to show how a place is captured first-hand, before its impressions are shaped and steered, cut and cleaned and made ready for reading. If you have no especial interest in uncensored blocks of reportage, and no especial interest in Newcastle, I advise you skip a few pages to Durham, where I resume a more orthodox approach.

I checked-in at the Albatross hostel on Grey Street; spent an hour or so in the hostel's communal lounge watching people fiddle prosaically with assorted devices. The hostel was purportedly full – I only got a room because of a cancellation – but there was scant evidence of the fact in its communal areas. Hostels used to be about bonhomie and bon vivant and other things beginning with bon-, their kitchens and lounges and dormitories thick with questions and chat and exchange. The first things I was issued upon checking-in at the Albatross were food labels and a padlock, and with them the implicit encouragement to guard and privatise rather than share and trust.

I went out to see the city, to call on its bars and cafes for beer and wine and crème de menthe, to pause against its old, cold buildings and wonder if the appellation *flâneur* was coined to console people with nowhere to go.

At the venerable Tyneside Cinema, I took advantage of a free screening of a tragicomedy called *Election*, wherein a college teacher's career and marriage fall apart after he rigs a student election and gets stung in the eye by a wasp.

On nearby Pilgrim Street, where I dutifully went, the remains of another cinema sit next to a gruesome office block in its forties. Newcastle's mix of buildings says something about the 20th century, about its early confidence and imperial egoism, its various tussles and concessions and booms and busts, and its later efforts to cut corners, to make do, to merely function.

On Northumberland Avenue a dull stretch of anywhere shops were winding down for the day, while on Shakespeare Street there's a coffeehouse called 9 Bar where the espresso machine is old and the music older and the staff serve robust Peruvians and pork shoulder milk buns wearing reading glasses and Brylcreem.

The Eldon Square Shopping Centre had me scratching my head. I asked a fellow *flâneur* how it happened. She said that the best-looking part of Newcastle – its neo-classical centre – was developed in the 1830s by a guy called Grainger. A portion of this best-looking centre was demolished in the 1960s to make space for the acre of awfulness in front of me, which, she said, was a criminal development as well as an ugly one. How so? Well, she went on, the council bigwig who oversaw the redevelopment of Grainger Town was found to be taking bungs from a property developer. Both bigwig and developer were sent to the local prison, which, ironically, was one of the former's final commissions.

Bryson liked Newcastle's buildings, considering many of them 'relics of genius and enterprise', which is certainly one way of looking at them. Another way to look at them is as relics of sweat and exploitation. When we see Grey Street, or Salisbury Cathedral, or the Tyne Bridge, or Blackpool Tower, we tend to see elegance and triumph rather than bad wages and toil. Why? Because it's easier to do so. To look at a building and see all that went into it – all the time, sweat, stress, exploitation, enrichment, genius, enterprise – is challenging and time consuming, and the rewards of doing so are nebulous, and so we don't bother.

And that is fair enough. Imagine if every time you encountered something (a building, a Kit Kat, a T-shirt) you paused to consider all of its determinants, all of its ingredients, all of its shaping factors. You wouldn't get far, would you? You'd be ten hours in Tesco doing a shop, and you'd be rubbish at going for a quick walk.

Instead, we take things at face value, for what they are, and remain ignorant of their long provenance, of their laborious journey. This course of action certainly makes life less bothersome, but it also renders us somewhat complicit in the sweat and the tears, the death and the glory, the loss and profit. So it goes.

Across the Tyne to Gateshead and The Baltic Gallery, once a flour mill, now a centre for contemporary art, where I enjoyed the work of Thomas Bayrle, whose satirical compositions are formed of hundreds of identical smaller parts, conjoined in such a way so as to portray another image. One of Bayrle's works showed a man using a smart phone. The work's smaller individual elements – its particles – were all tiny phones, gesturing to the worrying degree to which our phones constitute us, determine us, shape us, characterise us. If you remove the phone, runs the implication, you remove the being.

From the gallery's viewing platform on level five I saw the city from ahigh: on the Millennium Bridge bikers peddled, a busker fiddled, and commuters trod, all atop the dividing Tyne; on the quayside, queuing cars heeded the changing reds and greens and amber in-betweens; inland, I observed the turning hands of the clock of St Anne's; the old Co-op building, now a high-end hotel, pushing exclusive suites; a distant, once industrial, now strictly non-smoking chimney; and a stalled train outside the central station, waiting to run home our friends in the North.

Along a typically revived quayside to Ouseburn, where the old toffee factory now confects ad campaigns, and the Free Trade Inn calls for an end to the bedroom tax. I tried to find England's least-loved structure, the Byker Wall, but couldn't, not unless said wall is actually an estate of squat, angular council chalets. I had been warned about the Byker district. I had been warned the residents punch your face and pinch your device, no matter the quality of your protest. I passed through peacefully.

Back across the river and into The Sage, a shiny croissant-shaped concert hall that serves Jamie Cullum and Puccini. I was on time for evening carols, which I was unable to appreciate owing to the din of a hundred people enjoying end-of-week chat. Outside I met Sandy Duff, who runs The Sage's 'Learning and Participation' programme. It is Sandy's job to encourage local youngsters with antisocial pedigree to practice graffiti on council-sanctioned walls, so they can channel their boredom and angst in more creative ways. It is an odd gallery that Sandy curates. Not only does it stand in brilliant, subversive contrast to its large shiny neighbour, where the art is classical and taken with wine, but its exhibitions are definitively ephemeral, liable at any moment to be erased or undone.

Sandy told me that since the graffiti academy's funding was cut by 80 per cent, antisocial behaviour in the area had doubled, putting costly and avoidable strain on the police. Sandy then put forth some ideas for reforming the education system that carried far more common sense than anything recent ministers have managed, and he did so with great articulacy and in a tracksuit. British politics could do with a cabinet of Sandys.

Growing steadily more lonesome, I entered a cafe on Grey Street where poetry was being read and music being played. Of the poems I heard, I liked two in particular. One, by Daniel Smith, was a rhyming love letter to Hereford – 'Our Odeon cinema has only got one screen / And the city's flag is a cow by a stream' – and the other, by Rowan McCabe, a rhyming portrait of an archetypal Geordie called Billy Big Balls, whose manly bravado papers over a cracked and troubled child.

The 24-bed dormitory was quiet when I settled to sleep, but at two in the morning its calm was ruined when someone got in from a night out and made a noisy start on a kebab in the bunk below, opting to wash it down with something fizzy that prompted a very pop song of belches. I don't mind being woken when staying in a dorm – it's par for the course – but 45 minutes of noisy smelly kebab eating just wasn't cricket at all. But of course I put up with the noise because I'm English and the English are spineless and bite their tongues till they bleed.

Bryson went to Durham intending to poke around for an hour but fell in love with the place 'instantly and in a serious way' and so stayed for an hour and a half. He calls Durham a 'perfect little city', and couldn't believe that no one had told him about the place before, had never said, 'You've never been to Durham? Good God, man, you must go at once! Please – take my car.'

I had been to Durham once before, and I remember it being nice, being pleasant, but not 'perfect' by any means. For a start, there were far too many students wearing garments marked with their initials. Because Durham's students tend to have double-barrel surnames and at least two middle names, their hooded jumpers become pieces of loose-fitting literature, polyester statements of privilege, and thereby render Durham pleasant rather than perfect – in my book anyway.

Durham's castle is a thousand years old and sits high on a peninsula created by a meander in the River Wear. Because the castle is surrounded on three sides by steep, densely wooded riverbanks, it has proved perennially difficult to access. In fact, it is the only castle in the UK never to have suffered a breach; nineteen armies having tried and failed to enter without invitation.

The castle is now a university residence and I entered without invitation. Remembering how cheap it was to eat at my own university residence, I went directly to the dining room, which was wainscoted, high-ceilinged, and adorned with chandeliers and suits of armour and portraits of old white men looking surly.

Not knowing the local protocol, while everyone else helped themselves to silver spoons and fennel risotto, I could only stand amid all this confident activity with a dumb look on my face. Sensing a duck out of water, a dinner lady approached me.

'Can I help you?'

'No, I'm fine, thank you.'

'Are you in college?'

'Yes.'

'What block?'

'D.'

'Studying?'

'Gerontology.'

'Have you just arrived?'

'Yes. Just arrived. Clueless. Is there a salad buffet perchance?'

The dinner lady kindly indicated where the salad buffet was, before going on to commend the four-cheese dressing, explain what to do with my tray when I was finished, and wish me a pleasant and heavily subsidised four-course lunch. Perhaps Durham is perfect after all.

After lunch, I left the castle and made the short journey to the cathedral, a relatively junior establishment at only 960 years old. Inside, a school orchestra were in rehearsal for carols that evening. (Some of the instruments were larger than the musicians.) The rehearsal provided a nice soundtrack as I roamed the nave, transept, crypt or cloisters (I didn't know where I was and won't pretend that I did) and as I contemplated the stained-glass millennium window, with its down-to-earth panes showing industrial goings-on.

Elsewhere, in the nave, transept, crypt or cloisters, a Lego version of the cathedral was under construction. The building project, I was interested to learn, was already over budget and behind schedule. I would have happily gone up the cathedral's tower, but it was £5 to do so and I knew well that the city was presently interred in a mist, meaning Elvet Bridge and the Market Place and Gilesgate would all be temporarily under wraps. Instead, I read that in the Middle Ages the cathedral provided sanctuary for fugitives and heretics and coxcombs for a few weeks at a time, so they could organise their affairs and maybe become Christians. I thought about checking-in.

Bryson loved the cathedral for several reasons (its stout pillars, wooden pews, reddish-brown stone) but mostly because you don't have to tip. This adversity to gratuity is surprising given that Bryson is from America, where they tip their dogs every time they toilet on the sidewalk. Bryson's reluctance to tip could be seen as evidence of his comprehensive assimilation into British society. That's not to say you don't get grateful or generous people in Britain. Of course you do. They just don't tip so well. I worked in a restaurant in Portsmouth for about seven years and often waited on parties that would gush their thanks more or less constantly during the meal – after taking their order, after delivering their drinks, after taking their salt cellar for the use of another table – and then tip 60 pence.

It intrigues me that given his professed love for Durham, for this 'perfect little city', Bryson didn't choose to hang about longer. Perhaps this is a habit of his; perhaps Bryson is always in a rush when visiting the things he loves. When he visits his children, for example, I wonder if it's Bill's first task to announce that he can't stay for long because although he loves them dearly, and although they are perfect little children, and although he can't believe that no one had told him about them before ('You haven't seen your kids yet? Good God, man, you must go at once! Please – take my car'), he has to get to Scotland/Eastleigh/Alicante asap.

I crossed Elvet Bridge and walked to the university's students' union, where I asked a girl at an information point what foodstuffs were popular locally.

'Chips, pet.'

'Chips? Like …'

'Like chips, pet.'

'I suppose I mean what's unique to Durham? What would the miners have eaten?'

'Zen.'

'Zen?'

'It's a Thai restaurant. Me granda – he was a miner – says it's canny good but.'

'But what?'

'Ye wha'?'

'Never mind. So what's Durham like when the students go home?'

'Better.'

'What's the difference between northerners and southerners?'

'We sound thicker but are cannier like. Why ye asking so many questions?'

'Because this is an information point, pet.'

My next port of call was Ashington, a former mining village fifteen miles north. I took the X21 bus from Newcastle Haymarket and headed out of the city, skirting the grassy expanse of Town Moor. I read about the moor as it passed. I read that Newcastle's favourite people – its Freemen – are allowed to graze cattle on the moor, which is reasonable enough given how big it is and the fact that no one else seems to be doing anything with it.

Oddly though, the Freemen are also allowed to graze cattle on the pitch at St James' Park, the city's football stadium. Apparently this right is never exercised (though it can often seem otherwise; much of Newcastle's play last season spoke of cattle grazing). To thank the Freemen for not bringing their cows out during the Premier League season, each receives a small payment from the council, for loss of privilege or whatever. Bob Geldof – the guy who raised awareness of Africa – is one such Freeman. The idea of Geldof getting paid for not grazing cattle on the pitch at St James' Park pleases me very much, for I'm a big fan of the idea of wealthy people becoming wealthier still by doing nothing.

I'm also a big fan of the Ashington Group, a society of miner-painters founded in 1934 that met on Monday nights to depict life down the pit and in the surrounding areas. (One of the group's best-known works is of Geldof and his cow on the pitch at St James' Park.) The group attracted huge attention, and by the 1940s had earned a major reputation, enjoying exhibitions at the Tate and elsewhere. After the Second World War, however, membership numbers started to drop, and eventually the group disbanded in 1982, when the rent on the hut where they met went up from 50p a year to £14.[6]

Anyway, it was this hut – or the site on which the hut once stood – that Bryson came to Ashington to see. So after being put down by the X21 near Station Road, and after popping into Poundland to see what a quid got you these days (David Beckham calendar, non-stick roasting tin, kilo of broken shortbread), I spent about an hour stomping around in a steady Northumbrian drizzle trying to find a plot of land that used to be significant.

According to Bryson, the Ashington Group was 'regarded by critics and other aesthetes rather like Dr Johnson's performing dog', with the wonder being 'not that they did it well but that they did it at all'. I may be wrong, but I fear that a modern equivalent of the Pitmen Painters would be treated in much

---

[6] Their story really deserves a better account than I can offer here. Lee Hall tells it very well in his 2007 play *The Pitmen Painters*, which premiered in Newcastle before transferring to London's West End.

the same way, because the British class system still contrives to steer the working class toward certain careers and the middle and upper classes toward others. Thus, when there is a mix up, when a sheep breaks ranks and moves beyond the pale, it is a wonder to behold.

Some will argue that the above assertion is anachronistic baloney because social mobility has levelled the playing field, has given people of all social classes the opportunity to enter whatever profession they so choose. This is simply not the case. As previously argued, social mobility is at best unreliable and at worst fallacious. The playing field is anything but flat. And even if the playing field were flat, even if employers were class-blind and colour-blind and altogether unbiased, even if there was no rank nepotism, it's what happens *prior* to the playing field that is most crucial. It's what happens in the changing rooms, for example, when certain players are equipped with the tactics and nous to outsmart their opponents and others aren't. It's what happens in the back garden (if you've got one), where skills are honed and conferred. It's what happens in the local sports shop, where some players are taken to prepare for battle – pads, box, gloves, stick, spikes, helmet – and some are not. Given the above, the playing field being level is arguably beside the point.

Back to more important matters: walking along the Woodhorn Road towards the Colliery Museum, I was drawn into an innocuous Italian restaurant called Amaretto, which promised a three-course lunch for £4.95. In Blackpool my interest had been piqued by the promise of a five-course dinner for £10. I'm no mathematician, but three courses for a fiver seemed an even more eccentric proposition. I went inside and had mushroom soup followed by spaghetti bolognaise followed by vanilla ice cream, and it was all very good indeed. I told the waitress of my intention to eat at her restaurant once every five years until I died. 'In which case I hope I never see you again,' she said. I tipped her 50 per cent.

The Woodhorn colliery closed in 1981. It was one of 200 working pits in Northumberland alone, and of 3,000 in the country. Now there are none. After the colliery's closure it was made into a museum, and for this reason is like many of Britain's post-industrial sites, each smartly and swiftly archived, swept under the carpet and under new Lottery-funded roofs, to be gazed at rather than worked in.

Bryson enjoyed his gazing, mind you, and seems to have learned a great deal from his museum visit: that the Ashington Coal Company once employed 10,000 men; that these men, after clocking-off, would find the energy to frequent one of the many local cinemas and institutes and libraries and clubs that have all since gone up in smoke like the coal that bore them; that a thousand men a year died in the mines, and that each pit had a fabled disaster, which were often the result of criminally lax supervision on the part of the mine's owners, who, post-disaster, would receive no more than a slap on the wrist for their murderous negligence; that children as young as four would pull thirteen-hour shifts in the mines, which although not great for the kids certainly resolved any child-minding issues for the parents.

Leaving the museum, Bryson learns one more thing. He learns that the principal beneficiary of all the deadly underground effort carried out in Ashington was the fifth Duke of Portland, W.J.C. Bentinck, the guy in Worksop who built the underground mansion despite already having a perfectly good one above ground. In effect, then, if all those kids hadn't pulled all those thirteen-hour shifts, and all those men hadn't spent their vital years pulling up coal, the duke would never have got his underground mansion or his tunnels or his wigs. It doesn't bear thinking about.

Evidently so, for Bryson doesn't think about it; doesn't, in his writing at least, suggest that it's somewhat regrettable that all those years of inhuman labour, all those fatalities, all those dark jobbing toddlers, were for the enrichment of a sociopathic aristocrat who did nothing, precisely nothing, to earn the right to such enrichment save for exiting the right womb at the right time. Having stumbled upon the coincidence – that it was Bentinck at the helm of Woodhorn – Bryson merely points out what 'a remarkably, cherishably small world Britain is'.

The coincidence inspired a different mood in me. I was reminded of what Priestley had written about industrial England. Priestley concedes that a country cannot grow rich without some suffering and disorder – 'cannot make omelettes without breaking eggs' – but fears that the prevailing economic system is prone to issuing 'far too many eggshells and too few omelettes'.

On the industrial North in particular, Priestley writes: 'It's as if the region had devoted a hundred years of its life to keeping gigantic sooty pigs. And the people who were choked by the reek of the sties did not get the bacon.' When it comes to Ashington, and the Woodhorn Colliery, it would appear that our old friend Bentinck took both the omelette and the bacon, and then the biscuit to boot, and ate the lot back at his underground pad in Worksop, leaving Ashington to evolve into just another post-industrial no-man's-land, scattered with the broken shells of fallen soldiers.

The arrangement that sees the few take so much for doing so little, and the many so little for doing so much, is a troubling one. And yet it persists, and persists, and persists. Hey-ho.

24

Edinburgh

Arriving at Edinburgh Waverley Station, I was unable to receive the city in the thoughtful, kindly way Bryson had, who noted the floodlit monuments and the commuters shuffling happily home to haggis and cock-a-leekie soup. Bryson has a knack, I am starting to notice, of softly sketching the texture and atmosphere of a place in one or two pithy opening sentences. I don't have such a knack, so I lean on his, and hope he doesn't mind.

I proceeded on foot to the Ceilidh-Donia, a semi-detached Victorian property in a quiet residential district in the south of the city. Upon arriving, I was disappointed to see that the proprietor of the hotel was doing nothing demonstrably Scottish. She wasn't listening to Irvine Welsh's *Trainspotting* on BBC Radio Scotland, or cutting sausage meat into squares, or knitting a kilt or tossing a caber. I might as well have been in England.

My room, though small, was very comfortable and had all the things vital to effective travel: biscuits, fizzy water, a hair-dryer. After washing with the fizzy water and exfoliating with the biscuits, I turned on my heels and took the Dalkeith Road north until Rankeillor Street, where Emma Morley lived as a student. I fell in love with Emma after four chapters of David Nicholls' novel *One Day*. As I passed her make-believe address, feeling stupidly lovelorn, I sang a few bars of that song from

My Fair Lady, when Freddy goes to Warwick Avenue or wherever to call on Audrey Hepburn.

I walked to Holyrood Park, home of Arthur's Seat, Edinburgh's photogenic volcano, now in retirement, happy to run a low temperature and bear a thousand daily feet. The ascent is taxing, no matter your physique. I passed a young boy halfway up moaning about the climb to his mother. 'Just think of the sense of achievement,' she told him. The young boy's reply – 'I don't *care* about the sense of achievement' – was fair enough.

The climb pays off though. From the top you can see the city in all its glory: the Forth Bridge's long red range; cruise ships slipping slowly in at Leith; the dark finger of Tron Kirk; a new financial zone west of the castle, where RBS are responsibly quartered; Calton Hill, one of the city's seven; the Royal Mile, that sloping aorta, jutting eastward from the castle's midriff and running down to the Palace of Holyrood, where the Queen comes each summer to illustrate her importance to Scotland by having a square-sausage sandwich in the rain. Make no mistake, the city looked good and old from up there, too good perhaps, and too old maybe. There was something inauthentic about it, something cinematic, something staged. Had Edinburgh been pickled, or coddled, or put under wraps since the turn of the 19th century? Where were those familiar northern scars? Did dirty industry not strike here as elsewhere? Did German bombs not fall?

The Royal Mile, to which I succumbed, is flanked by early high-risers, burnt-salmon tenements, whose bottom rung is given over to commercial objectives. There were several shops purporting to sell the 'Scottish Experience', which seems to be limited to the wearing of cashmere and the eating of shortbread.

At the Mile's end I came to what looked like a very large Vietnamese restaurant. It was in fact the Scottish Parliament building. Scotland didn't have its own parliament when Bryson was here in '94. It gained that burden in 1998, when the Scotland Act was passed, which entitled the country to manage its own affairs (single malt, kippers, extreme cloud cover), while such matters as defence, taxation and warmongering remained the responsibility of the UK Parliament in London.

Following Bryson, I went to St Andrew's Square in the New Town, that august grid of Georgian respectability, laid out in the 18th century to counter old town congestion, and give the emerging middle class some breathing space. On one corner of the square is a pub called Tiles, where Bryson drank a 'foolish' amount of beer. I would have foolishly followed suit, but the pub smelt awfully of fried fish and was full to bursting with whinnying tourist-types like me, and so I let it alone and returned to Princes Street, Edinburgh's main drag.

To Bryson's mind, Princes Street offered 'nothing but the usual array of chain establishments – Boots, Littlewoods, Virgin Records, BHS, Marks and Spencer, Burger King, McDonald's'. If Bryson was impatient with the predictability of the British high street twenty years ago, he'd be even more so now. Upon any such street in the country one is bound to face the same line-up of corporate concerns: Greggs, Nandos, Poundland, Carphone Warehouse, Tesco, Costa, Wetherspoon, O2.

I know such things are hard to measure with any great degree of accuracy, but it is certainly my impression that the range and nature of our consumptive habits has narrowed. We tend increasingly to shop at the same supermarkets, to eat at the same restaurants, to drink at the same pubs and bars, to stay in the same incorporated hotels, to see the same films at the same multiplexes, to watch the same cat videos and share them on the same smart phones.

Of course, there are independent antidotes to the corporate mainstream, but they are exceptions to the rule, game swimmers going against the social current. Should this bother us? Well, yes, for any narrowing of experience necessarily entails a narrowing of consciousness, that is, of the breadth and quality of one's character – hardly something to aspire to.

I entered McDonald's on Princes Street, where Bryson came for an Egg McMuffin and to have a mild altercation with the cashier regarding an apple turnover. After his muffin Bill steps outside into heavy rain, where he takes the decision to 'sprint' across the road to the Royal Scottish Academy. I concede that in any account of travel there are bound to be moments of exaggeration. One might overstate the gradient of a hill, the length of a bath, the depth of a concern, the heat of a chilli, the success of a joke. So much is admitted. But for a man whose idea of exercise is moving from one room of a hotel to another to claim to have 'sprinted' across Princes Street, Edinburgh, is to stretch truth too far. Significantly, having sprinted across the road to the RSA, Bryson doesn't go on to climb one of the gallery's Doric columns and then enter via a skylight. No, he shakes himself 'dry like a dog' before 'shuffling in'. Now that's more like it, that has the ring of truth about it, that's the Bill we know and love.

Having shuffled into the RSA, Bryson had a mind to acquire a picture, a gift for long-suffering Cynthia perhaps, only to find that they were all too expensive. When I stopped at the gallery, I thought it might be nice if *I* bought a picture for Cynthia, with the idea of delivering it to her on Christmas Eve, when, by my calendar if not theirs, I was due to have a beer and some potato salad with the Brysons at their place in Norfolk.

One picture caught my attention. It was titled *Dennis and Margaret* and depicted two dogs outside a corner shop. When I asked its price, I was told that if I had to ask then I couldn't afford it. Undeterred, I asked what they had for twenty quid and was directed to a blank space on the wall. There's nothing there, I said. 'Exactly. You can have that for twenty quid if you want.'

Time was passing, and night was coming, and rain was once more falling, so I hastened up the Lothian Road, enjoying as I did so its sybaritic mix of high and low amusements: next to a classical concert hall, for example, there is a strip club called G-String in C-Minor; and next to a gastropub pushing fillets of hake, there is an establishment called Grab Me Tatties, which even does a pre-theatre menu. The concert hall had clearly just called time, for the street was of a sudden full of well-dressed folk, dashing for taxis, discussing the tenor's open fly, the flautist's cold sore, the soprano's bum notes. I noted several men ducking into Tatties for a cheeky amuse-bouche.

I followed Bread Street's soft rise, cut through the Grassmarket, climbed the steep curve of Victoria Street until it met George IV Bridge, where I entered a bar called The Village. I spoke with the barman, a philosophy student with plans to be a freelance political analyst. I asked him about the upcoming referendum, about whether he was up for independence. He ran a hand through Harry-Styles hair before confessing that he hadn't really thought about it. I assured him that if he kept that up, he'd almost certainly become a political analyst, freelance or otherwise.

I went to Princes Street Gardens, where a Christmas market was in train. The market was replete with long sausages and apfelstrudel and mulled wine and mulled cider and mulled chicken soup and everything else that can conceivably be mulled. Lovers were ice-skating in orange boots, falling deeper into love with each tumble, happy with their bruises and their calamity, embracing to achieve balance, laughing freely. I tried to hire a pair of skates so I could join the lovers on the ice and, by osmosis perhaps, absorb some of their happiness and pride and longing.

I bought a large tray of chips and made my way home, quickly along Nicolson and Clerk, slowly on Rankeillor. Remembering the lovers on the ice rink, and remembering Emma Morley, it occurred to me that Edinburgh was a city to fall in love in, to hold hands in, to decide on life's project in, to invent in, to emerge in. Something of the city's scale and beauty and heritage and epic topography must find its way into the daydreams of its people, its small, fleeting, ordinary people, who walk its streets and cross its bridges and skirt its puddles with a spring in their step, sensing that all is possible.

A quick look at the city's CV bears this out. Alexander Graham Bell sorted out the telephone in Edinburgh; James Hutton, the so-called 'Father of Geology', invented a branch of knowledge here; Ian Wilmut cloned a sheep; Peter Higgs sought the God particle; J.K. Rowling begot Potter on a dodgy laptop near the castle; Stevenson gave his Jekyll and Hyde, Hogg his Justified Sinner, Conan Doyle his Holmes. What a company! What alumni! Can you imagine that lot meeting at a student house party? Can you imagine them filling the tiny kitchen, having a go at small talk?

'So, James, what do you do?'

'I'm a single parent.'

'Boy or girl?'

'Geology actually. And you?'

'I'm trying to come up with something that will allow anybody in the world to speak to anybody else in the world. Drink?'

The chips went on and on, and were somehow improved by the light, undaunted drizzle, which made the cheap mayonnaise go thinner and further, and helped form an unlikely rainwater-vinaigrette at the bottom of the tray. As I ate the pulpy odds and ends, I wondered what I could boast of if I were at such a party, in such bright company, with Bell and Doyle and Rowling and Higgs. The answer was little.

25

Aberdeen–Inverness

The Mariner Hotel was very nice, which disappointed me. To respect Bryson's example, I had wanted to stay in a 'dreary, overpriced backstreet block', but when I searched online for hotels in Aberdeen I couldn't find any that matched that description, and so opted for the Mariner and hoped for the worst, only for the place to let me down by some margin. The receptionist at the hotel must have been a bit confused when I asked if he had a room that was damp and ill-lit.

After a quick nap and some green tea I walked back into town, hoping to find it more likable than Bryson had. On Gray Street – aptly named I must say – I noted a schoolboy coming the other way. He was kicking a football about as he made his way up the street. As he drew closer to me I asked for a 'quick one-two', meaning that he should pass the ball to me and I would quickly pass it back, only the kid played a sloppy pass into my left foot, which is my weaker, giving me no choice but to punt the ball into a parked Volvo.

'Sorry mate. I'm English.'

'Aye and ye can stay English.'

It wasn't long before Aberdeen started to demonstrate its healthy GDP, to wear its wealth on its sleeve. Up and down the clean streets went large cars driven by moisturised men in decent knitwear. Even the buildings appeared to moisturise. They certainly had a youthful complexion. In a gluten-free bakery it was explained to me that granite is slow to show signs of age, with the result that Aberdeen looks as juvenile as the day it was put up. It's the Peter Pan of British cities.

At the west end of Union Street, the 'No to Scottish Independence' campaign was headquartered in a forgotten shoe shop. Before I could open my mouth I was offered a handful of sweets by a neuroscience graduate, which did little to clarify why Scotland was better off in the United Kingdom, but much to endear me to the campaign. The graduate told me that most people were still unsure what an independent Scotland would look like (would it retain the pound, or EU membership, or *The Archers*?), but that she definitely had some gobstoppers out the back if I wanted one.

More persuasive than the graduate's saccharine propaganda was the conflicting jingoism I noticed around Union Terrace Gardens, a charming subterranean park near the train station. At the meeting point of Union Street and Union Terrace there is a statue of Edward VII, before which a kilted man played William Blake's *Jerusalem* on the bagpipes. Meanwhile, on the north side of the gardens, *Macbeth* was having a run at His Majesty's Theatre. And on a bench on the east side of the gardens, two teenage girls – one in a Scotland football shirt, the other with a Union Jack mobile phone cover – discussed the travails of being young. There was a pleasant and peaceful disunity around that garden, and it seemed to whisper support for the status quo.

Broad Street's greatest burden is Marischal College. But what a burden! It is a vast, ashen building, the type children build from blocks in their dreams to house this or that wizard-king. The building used to be part of the university but is now occupied by the local council. In the building's foyer, a display gave the results of a recent public consultation regarding a multi-purpose civic space due to be built on top – yes, *on top* – of Union Terrace Gardens. Snippets of the public's feedback were displayed in enthusiastic speech bubbles. By my reckoning, the council are going to have a tough job keeping everyone happy, for the public's feedback made such contradictory reading. How for example does the council intend to have lots of glass and none at all; have plenty of open space and nowhere that thugs might congregate; and to use local granite and something different for a change?

At a butcher's shop on Justice Street I sampled a 'mince and mealie' pie, which ought to be served with a pint of gravy, so dry is the pie's filling. When the butcher told me there was a sandy beach and a funfair about a kilometre away, I said he'd already played one joke on me by selling me that pie so he ought to think twice before playing another.

There was a sandy beach and a funfair about a kilometre away, notwithstanding the fact that Aberdeen is statistically the coldest place in the UK. The funfair is called Sunset Boulevard, which I suppose it can just about get away with. It has arcades, roller coasters and a water slide, and was surely the most daring project to be undertaken in Scotland since the Highland clearances. Who on earth put money into it? Probably the local council, following a public consultation.

The beach is no trifle either; it runs for several miles, between the Dee and Don rivers. I stood on the esplanade and watched an afternoon moon turn up between oil tankers.

Aberdeen used to fish for cod and herring: now it trawls for the black stuff. The first major discovery of oil here was in 1970, a hundred miles off the coast. Five years of hard work later and the ghastly infrastructure necessary to draw oil was ready, which illustrates just how quickly an economy can adapt to new energy sources when it wants to. Now the industry supports 50,000 jobs, a quarter of the city's population.

I went south on the esplanade to the retired fishing village of Footdee, a modest grid of small stone houses whence shoals of seamen would once have emerged each lightless morning to hunt mackerel. Next door to Footdee is Aberdeen's commercial harbour, a colossal junction where the oil tankers offload their catch. The scale of the harbour reveals the scale of the oil game: every year a billion barrels are lifted from 11,000 wells by 900 energy companies. Oil is to Aberdeen what cotton was to Manchester, what wool was to Bradford, and what coal was to Ashington. And like the cotton, wool and coal, oil too has a shelf life. And where will Aberdeen be then? Will it have to forego its funfair? Will its evergreen granite finally begin to waver? I asked a Lancastrian climbing a giant silo if he was worried that Aberdeen was a one-trick pony. 'Better one trick than none, cocker.'

Bryson went to an Indian restaurant for dinner and so did I. Inside The Jewel in the Crown, the smell of oil was unmistakable. The waiters wore Ralph Lauren and the patrons were dressed to present the weather. The dinner talk was pretty crude as well: it was all barrels per minute and what time last orders were at the Suez Canal. I looked at the menu and quickly realised that I wasn't going to get three courses for a fiver. Before I had even figured out how to open the menu the waiter had delivered a saucer of orange slices and a hot flannel, which I pretended to mistake for a starter. At the adjoining table I noticed a well-heeled woman, evidently nouveau-riche, attempting to eat a poppadom with cutlery. It was a funny place, and my last memory of Aberdeen.

Bryson liked Inverness immediately; I liked it eventually. Inverness is Britain's northernmost city and famous for punch-ups, the most significant of which was the Battle of Culloden in 1746, which put an end to the second Jacobite Rising, which saw a bunch of highlanders recruit Bonnie Prince Charlie from AC Milan to play centre forward in the rabble's southward charge to London, where the idea was to dethrone whoever was on the throne by any which way.

I was sad to learn that the city has settled down a bit of late. Indeed, a recent survey revealed that Inverness is the second happiest settlement in Britain. A contributor to happiness levels must be the strength of the local economy, which ballooned between 1997 and 2008, when the locals ended their centuries-long attempt to find the Loch Ness monster and started doing standard nine-to-five jobs instead.

Bryson doesn't offer the name of his hotel in Inverness, so I was once more obliged to stay where I wished, or if not where I wished then where I could wrangle a fair price. After complimenting the tartan carpet that dominates the hotel's reception area, I managed to cut a deal at the Craigmonie on Annfield Road. I dumped my bag and then headed impatiently to the basement, where there was a gym and swimming pool and sauna, which had clearly been introduced in the 80s and then left alone for 30 years. Everything was pleasingly small-scale: the sauna was large enough to host a single large person or two slight ones, and the pool was more suitable for birthing than swimming. If not looking younger, I at least emerged from my spa session somewhat reduced.

First on my to-do list was the city's sandstone castle, now a collection of law courts overlooking the broad green River Ness. I had a look in the Defence Witness Room, and then one of the larger courtrooms, where I had a mind to put myself on trial for general incompetence.

Next on the list was the indoor Victorian market on Academy Street, which has retained its old-fashioned barber-shop and its joke shop and its effortless evocation of 1953. The joke shop had been closed when Bryson visited but I had no such luck. It's less a shop and more a ludic archive of inappro-priate props, marshalled charismatically, and with the sobriety of a librarian, by Nancy, who's been flogging funny stuff for 60 years.

Nancy and I got off on the wrong foot when she caught me photographing her collection of 'Swimming Dicks'. In an effort to regain Nancy's confidence, I asked a few harmless questions about her business, including what her bestseller was. 'Dog poo, of course.' I bought two kilos, hoping that by making such a crap purchase Nancy might forgive me for snapping her dicks. Not a chance. 'I don't care to know what you're want-ing all that for,' Nancy said. 'You've plainly too much time on your hands.'

I walked through a district called Merkinch towards the Caledonian Canal. The canal was built in the late 18th century to allow fish caught in the east to be eaten with chips fried in the west, and vice versa. Beside the canal is Stan Fraser's Titanic Museum, which is dominated by a 100-foot replica of that unfortunate ship. I drank a cup of tea in the ship's smoking room, while watching key moments from the 1953 dramatisation of its sinking starring Clifford Webb. Much is made of Britain being a land of eccentrics and hobbyists (most travel writers suggest as much), but to be honest I haven't seen much of that sort of thing. Stan Fraser is certainly an eccentric hobbyist, though, and his museum is a fantastic treat and a relief to the spirit, particularly after spending twenty humourless minutes at Nancy's joke shop.

At the end of the canal, where the River Ness meets the Moray Firth and a cordon of frigid mountains, my humour started to worsen. I had drunk too much and had slept too little of late, and this rotten combination was beginning to spoil my mood. Despite the obvious beauty of the vista before me, Inverness was struggling to impress me. Indeed, I was starting to wonder what had been put in Bill's porridge the morning he walked around the city and considered making it his home. I'd sooner live in Bradford or Aberdeen, settlements that Bryson had little time for.

Resisting the temptation to call it a day and return to the hotel, I tracked the river for a few miles in the fading light. I took a moment to escape the cold in the Eden Arts Centre. The centre is apparently the biggest of its kind in the country, and offers a theatre and a pair of cinemas, one of which, La Scala, is named after the independent picture house that Bryson considered one of the city's most likable features. Bryson's good opinion wasn't sufficient to save the cinema, however. It was pulled down in 2001 after losing trade to an out-of-town multiplex. So it goes.

I persisted along the river until I came to a group of small islands accessed by a Victorian suspension bridge. It had long since been dark and the islands were as deserted as Crusoe's. Nonetheless, I wasn't at all apprehensive and that didn't surprise me, for one doesn't tend to experience fear on the road. Because Inverness was new to me, because I hadn't suffered here, or been frightened or victimised, the city was perfectly innocent, perfectly safe. I stopped on a bridge to stare at the busy gallons charging eastward to the open firth. I made a harsh pillow of the bridge's rail and wondered with brief sincerity what would become of me if I were to put myself in the water and go along with the gallons. I never would have, but the idea was real and lucid and reasonable, and thus a reminder of how fragile all this is, how close is the 'solving emptiness' dreamt of by Larkin.

I asked at a Cornish pasty shop on the high street if seeing as they were about to close they might discount something, but they said they didn't do that sort of thing, and so I spent my final £2 on brioche and salt and vinegar crisps, which I ate down by the river before drifting heavily back to the hotel.

26

Thurso

On the train to Thurso, I was issued a menu which ran to seven pages. When Bryson rode an equivalent train in '94, he was impressed that he could get a sandwich that didn't make him puke, which he took as irrefutable evidence that British Rail had come a long way since the 70s. British Rail is no more of course. Rightly or wrongly, the network was sold off piecemeal to private companies not long after Bryson's valedictory tour in 1994. I studied the seven-page menu with the patience of a man with little to do for the next five hours: toffee waffles, chinois, Thai sweet-chilli nuts, dessert wine. If an effect of privatisation is toffee waffles, I thought, sell the whole country if you must.

I kept an eye open for those markers dropped by Bryson – pebbledash bungalows, round mountains, cold nothingness – and dropped some of my own: dark orange cattle, frigid sheep, hopeful solar panels, the surprising palette of the landscape, with its auburn and lime and chalk and cheese and tungsten and tobacco. At Golspie the seldom sun burst through the blinds to fill the carriage daringly, as if sensing that it had but a few minutes before it would be veiled once more; and at Georgemas Junction it was announced that the driver would be 'changing ends' – for a laugh, I suppose.

Bryson wondered what all the people did for work in the sleepy settlements in the north of Scotland – at Golspie and

Brora for example – and so I asked the guard on the train. There isn't a great amount of work, I was told, particularly for the young people, who invariably move away to Thurso and Wick, and occasionally to Inverness to work as interns at Nancy's joke shop. I asked if a lot of the families require support from the State, in the form of housing benefit or job seeker's allowance, but he insisted that that wasn't really the case, that most were self-sufficient to an extent, with a generator for electricity and an allotment. He told me that he was from London but had been living up here for six years and wouldn't dream of going back. 'In London I lived next door to the same bloke for ten years and didn't know his name. And I didn't think that was odd. Here I've got to walk a mile to their houses, but I know everyone and count them as friends. It's happier.'

After checking-in at the Pentland Hotel in Thurso, which Bryson considered 'nice enough in an end-of-the-world sort of way', I did the usual things one does when familiarising oneself with a hotel room. First I read everything – the breakfast menu, the safety information, the instructions for the fire extinguisher, the labels on the soap and slippers. Then I sampled everything – any biscuits, fruit, long-life milk, mints. Then I sat everywhere – the armchair, the desk, the bed, the window-sill, the toilet. And finally I checked everything – the bedside lamp, the shower, the phone, the mini-bar, the toilet's flush, the curtains' pull, the slippers' fit, the TV's channels. Once satisfied that all was well for the time being, I went out to have a look at the town.

Thurso is a gentle, inoffensive sort of place: by no means is it preparing a bid to host the Olympics. The town gives the impression of not having changed a great deal over the past few hundred years – independent shops, quiet streets, old stone – which is fine if the place was generally agreeable a few hundred years ago, but regrettable if it wasn't.

Because I had caught a later train than anticipated, I had just half an hour in Thurso before I had to catch a bus to John O' Groats, twenty miles to the northeast and famous for being, well, twenty miles to the northeast. In that half an hour I wanted to see the ruined castle alluded to by Bryson, and so asked in a housing association office on Traill Street where it might be found. Perhaps the person I asked failed to understand my southern accent, for I was directed to a Norman church in the town centre, Old St Peter's, which wasn't what I was after but was diverting in any case.

I learned that the church also used to serve as a sort of criminal court, and that in 1701 the church decided that a local woman who had been caught having a fling with a Dutch sailor should be punished by having her head shaved and being paraded through town by the local hangman, presumably to warn the townspeople of the dangers of carrying-on with the Dutch. Oh the good old days when the church was also the judiciary! For God's sake, I hope this country is never so short-staffed again.

I found the ruined castle down by the beach, about 500 metres east of a fish warehouse. It was quite wonderful in a disappointing kind of way, it being a bleak sort of pleasure seeing such a building in an active state of disrepair. An old lady with a dog pulled up beside me. 'It was once a bonny place,' the lady said, before falling quiet.

After a time, the lady turned to me once more and explained softly that she had recently lost her husband, and that the loss had been tempered by her dog who, despite being discouraged from doing so, continued to sleep at the end of her bed. She pointed to the brave surfers out on the loud waves of Thurso Bay, and then to Scrabster Harbour where a little fishing goes on but not as much as before. The lady had that Caithness accent that Bill so rightly described as clinically precise and yet dulcet. They must make excellent readers of poetry these Highlanders, and convincing politicians.

The bus to John O' Groats was full of homeward school-children, whose accents were less precise and less dulcet than the old lady by the sea. What's more, the kids' speech was full of adolescent shortcuts like 'whatevs' and 'obvs', the former used to express indifference, and the latter both indifference and agreement.

It wasn't only the sound of their talk that bothered me, but the nature of it. One would expect the children of Thurso and its environs to have a more bucolic and rarefied set of concerns, but, alas, no. If there was a single moment when any of the fifteen conversations going on about me drifted away from one of two things – cider and *Britain's Got Talent* – then I sadly missed it. Where was the discussion of salmon fishing, or the preservation of the Gaelic language, or the pros and cons of living with a nuclear reactor in your back yard?

When Bryson passed along this road in a hired Ford Thesaurus he noted an arresting landscape of 'billowy, winter-bleached grass running down to a choppy sea and the hazy Orkneys beyond'. Well, I take your word for it, Bill, because I could see sod all. Not only was it already dark, but the local children were climbing all over the seats and blocking the windows. Despite their generally diabolical behaviour (I was tempted to shave their heads and parade them through town), I felt some sympathy for those children dropped off in the most unlikely spots. One girl was put down at the edge of six acres of cold scrubby farmland, without a dwelling in sight. She set off toward the choppy sea and the timorous moon. What was this kid, a troglodyte?

John O' Groats is pretty disappointing to be honest. Its only redeeming feature is that there isn't much of it. There's a car-park and an ice cream kiosk and a gift shop selling postcards, sweaters and videos by a singer named Tommy Scott, who Bryson was particularly underwhelmed by. Normally there's a decent view, of course, but it was pitch black so I couldn't see a thing. Indeed, the only clue that I was at a threshold of any kind was the persistent sound of waves. If this was the end of the road, it could stay at the end of the road.

Bryson spent his time at Britain's terminus watching three elderly women folding jumpers and pricing postcards. Because it was early evening when I arrived, the shop was starting to close. The shop's supervisor said that I could come in but that I mustn't linger. I was in the shop long enough to find a stack of Tommy Scott DVDs, the most recent of which included the tracks 'Will Ye Come Tae Ma Party' and 'Will Ye Go Lassie Go', which sound like the pleas of a lovelorn teenager caught in two minds.

I left the shop and walked into the teeth of a spiteful wind back to the bus stop. Next to the bus stop stands a lonely white hotel. God only knows who takes a room here. Maybe Tommy Scott when he's in the area shooting a music video. It was below freezing outside and my bus wasn't due for twenty minutes, and so I went in for a dram. The barmaid was being heckled mercilessly by a guy about to begin a shift at the nuclear reactor. The heckling had to do with the girl's suntan, which was obviously improvised. 'Ye look like Frank Bruno,' the man suggested. 'Are ye not worried that you'll be the only girl in Caithness with a tan?' The girl gave this some thought. 'Nah. Shannon's got one too.'

Back in Thurso and with little else to do, Bryson began asking himself a series of tough questions, like why it's called a jumper, and why it's called a grapefruit? To plug his 'interrogative diarrhoea', Bill knew that he needed a forceful distraction, which he found in the shape of the Fountain Restaurant, which offered three cuisines (Chinese, Indian and European) under one roof. Bill was 'immediately taken with this concept', but then struggled to choose between the three. In the end, and for the eleventh time in 27 chapters, Bryson goes for Chinese, a rate of consumption that would kill most children. I don't wish to be unkind, but Bryson must have put on quite a bit of weight during his trip (I know I did). Indeed, I wouldn't be surprised if Cynthia, upon her husband's return to the family home, failed to recognise the guy. 'Okay kids, stay calm. Woodrow, pass me a bread knife. Beyoncé, call the police. Tell them there's a large man from Shanghai in the house claiming to be my husband.'

Bryson's verdict on the food at The Fountain, for the record, was that it tasted like Chinese food cooked by a Scot, which was fine by Bill, because 'at least it was different, and that, by this stage of the trip, was all I craved'. If difference was all you craved Bill, then why in the name of the Virgin Mary did you order Chinese again?

I was due on the 8 o'clock train to Glasgow the next morning, so permitted myself just the one drink at the hotel bar before going to bed. The barman told me a few things about the nuclear facility up the road: that the local population tripled when it was established 60 years ago; that the facility was decommissioned in the late 90s when it was discovered that nuclear waste was dodgy after all; and that owing to coastal erosion the 65-metre deep shaft used for storing nuclear waste is due to collapse into the sea in 300 years' time, an event that will see local properties become affordable for young buyers for the first time since 1984.

I suggested that Thurso had pulled the short straw, therefore; that the town had been shafted. 'Yes and no. Thurso has done all right out of the nuclear plant. It's a wager, I suppose: here's work for thousands but if shit hits the fan you better make sure your bike's not got a puncture.' Call me macabre, but I quite like the idea of the population of Thurso – particularly its schoolchildren – rallying south in the wake of a nuclear catastrophe.

The night before his departure, Bill asked the kindly lady at the Pentland for a wake-up call at 5. To Bill's astonishment, the lady's response was to ask if he'd like a cooked breakfast in the morning before he set off. My train wasn't as early as

Bill's. I didn't have to be up until 7 and could take breakfast at a more conventional time. But I thought I'd pretend that the situation was otherwise, that I had to go salmon fishing before dawn and would therefore require a cooked breakfast just after 5, just to see if the hotel was as accommodating now as it was then.

And so, before retiring to bed, I asked the equivalent kindly lady at the Pentland if I could have a cooked breakfast just after 5. The equivalent kindly lady looked at me unkindly and said: 'Aye, nae bother, Mr Aitken. Ah'll get the chef to do it now and then leave it outside your room.'

27

Glasgow

For the second morning in a row I ate soft-boiled eggs in the relative dark. It was hard to tell the yolk from the white. Once more I tried to read a newspaper, but registered nothing save that the local football team are called The Vikings and the local college now offers degrees in nuclear decommissioning. What is it about the hours before dawn that are so heavy? I remembered Larkin's poem *Aubade* – 'slowly light strengthens, and the room takes shape' – then tried Marmite for the first time. I was deeply unsure. Something told me it was time to go home.

I was more or less alone at Thurso station. There were certainly no members of staff, which was a nuisance because I had intended to collect my pre-paid ticket from the station office. Aware that the ScotRail guards were a fussy bunch, quick to give fines and slow to cut slack, I boarded the train apprehensively. But I needn't have worried, because the guard was anything but fussy. In fact he seemed determined to do the least amount of work possible, preferring to issue wisdom rather than punishment. 'The road to hell is paved with good intentions, pal,' he said. 'Just ye remember tha'.'

The journey south was undramatic, restful even. The slowly rushing landscape had a palliative effect. There was just so much of it – station after station, acre after acre, frame after frame. The sum of all that goes by on a train is a sublime thing, and sublime things have a beneficent habit of making us feel small and slight, of exposing our ordinary concerns – bills, boys, business – for what they are. Train slideshows underline the mad extent of existence, and do us a favour thereby.

As well as feeling slight and small I also felt sad. I was coming to the end of things. After Glasgow, you see, Bryson took a train to Carlisle and then another to Skipton, where he was collected by his beloved Cynthia and taken home to his family. So I knew that as far as the retracing was concerned I was pretty much through. I had a few things to do in Glasgow, of course, and there would be a 'refreshing cup of coffee' at Carlisle, but very little besides.

I'm tempted to overstate the degree of my sadness for literary effect – to create a funereal atmosphere in which the latter pages of this book can poignantly unfold – but I won't because I wasn't as sad as all that. Relative to other experiences – a burst appendix, eating alone at KFC, Ebola – I knew well that my having to leave Bryson's side and get on with my own life was a very soft affliction.

But it was an affliction nonetheless, and so to cheer myself up a little I played a game, one of Bryson's favourites, wherein he makes a mental list of all the people he would love to watch being eaten alive by rabid dogs, a list that tended to include the person in charge of escalator maintenance at Heathrow Airport and the local councillor who petitioned for the closure of the Chinese takeaway in Bill's village.

My own list, in case you're interested, included the bald guy who took six years to order ham in Monmouth; the chap in Newcastle who ate a kebab in the bunk below; the book-keeper who encouraged me to back Morecambe to win 4–0;

every schoolchild in Thurso; the bloke who gave me directions in Newmarket then ran off after his dog without saying goodbye; the hotelier in Blackpool who reckons that steamed vegetables count as a course; the woman who tried to eat a poppadom with cutlery; whoever installed the voice-activated lighting system in the bridal suite at Rudding Park Hotel; the guy who shot someone in the Falklands because they didn't have Assam tea; the kid in Aberdeen who played a sloppy pass into my weaker left foot; Rupert Goodness-Gracious and his PhD on Jane Austen; whoever commissioned Europe's largest outdoor paddling pool in Bradford; and Nancy.

Just to be fair, I then had considerably less fun thinking of all the people that I definitely *did not* want to be eaten alive, people like Rita in Morecambe; the woman who give me £10 in Salisbury so I could buy myself a decent meal; Stan Fraser and his Titanic Museum; the couple who lovingly appraised each item of their cooked breakfast five days on the trot; the old lady by the sea who recently lost her husband; the young lad who gave me a free sausage in Newmarket; Ken Barlow; Steve and his dog in Retford; the guy who looked like Fagin and offered me hashish in Dorset; the chef at the Kashmir in Bradford; Wyn Rees, who broke his pelvis and got divorced on the same day on two occasions; the professional Santa in Blackpool; whoever came up with the name G-String in C-minor.

The lists I drew up were more or less the same length. To suggest that Britain is equal parts good and bad would be very unfair indeed. The truth is that the list of people to celebrate could have gone on and on and on, whereas the list of people to slay was, at heart, a bogus one. I don't wish Nancy ill. I just don't wish her well, that's all.

Arriving at Glasgow's Queen Street Station in 1973, Bryson was struck by how soot-blackened the city's once-bright buildings appeared, and how few tourists there were. Back then, says Bill, Glasgow wasn't even mentioned in his *Let's Go* guide to Europe. Things were different when he returned in '94, however – the buildings had been spruced, socks pulled up, tourists invited – and things are even more different now. Despite some chronic social problems, Glasgow is now considered by *Lonely Planet* to be one of the ten best tourist cities in the world, which is quite a turnaround.

If Glasgow's transformation from sooty 70s ghetto to one of the world's preferred holiday destinations was impressive, so was the city's transformation from a 17th-century backwater to a major metropolis with a world-ranking turnover. The city's commercial fortunes picked up after the invention of America, which became a major trading partner, and then things got even busier after Glasgow did well in the Enlightenment, during which time it learned to make bridges, cigarettes, ships, carpet, furniture, garments, deep-fried pizza and, of course, a hell of a mess.

Hard times were brought by the Great Depression of the 1930s, and then after the Second World War the city experienced further decline and gradual de-industrialisation, other nations having learned the tricks Glasgow learned a century before. The last 30 years have seen an effective diversification of the local economy, as well as investment in culture and infrastructure, which has once more lifted the city's mood and reputation. As Bryson notes, when the city was named Capital of Culture in 1990 no one laughed. And nor did they laugh when it was announced that Glasgow would host the Commonwealth Games in 2014, at which Bryson was due to compete in such events as How Long Can You Keep Your Jacket On.

One of the best recent additions to the city, says Bryson, is the Burrell Collection, a group of 8,000 artworks bequeathed to Glasgow by a local shipping magnate called William Burrell, and to which Bryson hastens after checking-in at his unnamed hotel. I didn't hasten to the Burrell Collection because I had to wait for my friend Andy to arrive at Queen Street on the London train. Andy and I became good friends while at university, having been housed next door to each other in our first year. Andy began university a teetotal Christian, and I would often drop into his room for sober advice as to how I might convince someone called Robin that I was far more attractive than I appeared. These early counselling sessions proved the bedrock of a long and ongoing friendship.

When Andy emerged from the ugly stomach of Queen Street Station an hour later, we went directly to our guesthouse near Kelvingrove Park. The guesthouse was faultless: I was instantly ready to move in; instantly ready to call my dad and have him send up my stuff from Portsmouth. I could jog in Kelvingrove Park, I fancied, and dine in the West End, and picnic on the hard shoulder of the M8, cleverly introduced to Glasgow's Victorian city centre in 1974.

As in Thurso, I spent twenty minutes nosing around the room, like a detective looking for clues. I can't tell you if the wardrobe was rococo, and I can't tell you if the sheets were Egyptian, but I can tell you that it was all pretty high-spec. It seemed the kind of place the BBC might use when in town making a documentary about relative poverty. Our room gave a view of a proud Victorian cityscape: the townhouses of Kelvingrove, the spire of the university, the tower of a church. I suggested to Andy that we be kind to ourselves and just hole-up for the evening, maybe watch one of his favourite films – *Miss Congeniality* – and get a takeaway. But he was having none of it. He knew that Bryson had gone out for a few pints at a rundown boozer and wanted very much to do likewise.

The Laurieston on Bridge Street, just south of the River Clyde, is not where you'd go for a cream tea. The pub is situated in one of Glasgow's former downtown slum districts. I say former because the district's Victorian tenements were comprehensively cleared or levelled in the decades after the Second World War, a period during which the population of Glasgow's city centre almost halved, as entire communities were copy and pasted from dark old inner-city slums to bright new outer-city ones.

The lack of infrastructure afforded the new housing estates led, unsurprisingly, to significant social problems. Accordingly, the new estates have a reputation for being somewhat rough and ready. The Glasgow comedian Kevin Bridges has a story about a twelve-year-old kid from such an estate. The kid is on holiday with his parents in Alicante. After refusing to get involved in a game of kids' water polo on account of having only just got in after a night out, the kid swims over to his dad and asks for a cigarette, saying that he's gasping. The mother is understandably horrified and tells the dad to address his son's behaviour. 'Aye,' goes the dad, 'aye, yer right. Anthony yer wee tube, ah've goat summin tae say tae yer: buy yer own fucking fags!'

We took pints of Tennent's to a distressed banquette and tried to tune into neighbouring conversations, remembering the difficulty Bryson had understanding the locals when he dropped into a similar pub twenty years before. On that occasion, one of the pub's regulars tried to get some chat going with Bryson by asking such questions as 'Hae ya nae hook ma dooky?' and 'D'ye hae a hoo and a poo?', which left Bryson scratching his head and wishing he were back in Des Moines picking corn.

For the benefit of future visitors to the city, Andy and I had a stab at translating some local phrases. We learned that 'Away wi ye mon, before ah stick the nut on ye' means clear off otherwise I'll damage your face; that 'Atspish' means I don't believe you; that 'Aye, the barras are barry' means the wheelbarrows are decent; that 'Ah goat these bits af the back o a lorry, yer baw bag' means I am wearing something stolen; that 'Every time I see Miliband's coupon ah wantae boak' means I'm not impressed with the Labour Party leader; and, last but not least, that 'Ah goat aff at Paisley' means I alighted at Paisley Gilmour Street, and is code for coitus interruptus.

Emerging from the pub, our minds turned to food. Andy knew that Glasgow was the vegan capital of the UK, and so felt that he ought to check out the local vegetable scene. I on the other hand wanted to sample a local delicacy – deep-fried pizza. I knew about deep-fried pizza because a couple of mates, soon to be married, had made a film about the stuff four years earlier (don't ask me why; they just did). The film presents deep-fried pizza in a positive light, which it shouldn't, because it's largely disgusting. It is obvious to any visitor that Glasgow is doing many things right these days – culturally, architecturally, commercially – but it really must, if it is to retain its place in *Lonely Planet*'s top ten, curb its enthusiasm for deep-frying things. Apart from pizza, the chip shops of Glasgow have been known to deep-fry chocolate bars, spam, eggs, cheeseburgers and English people. Even the two salmon that appear on the city's coat of arms appear to have been deep-fried. Enough is enough.

The next morning, before taking trains in different directions, Andy and I had time to visit the Burrell Collection. We took a bus to the edge of Pollok Park, about three miles south of the city centre, wherein the museum is situated. Bryson played a game while exploring the Burrell Collection. He pretended that the Scottish people had invited him to choose any item to take home as a gift, 'in recognition of his fineness as a person'.

With Andy lapping up a load of waffle about Impressionism elsewhere in the museum, I played the same game. After half an hour I had reduced the collection's 8,000 bits and pieces to a shortlist of three: an earthenware figure of an Uzbekistani man on his wedding day; a painting called *A Side Canal, Venice* by James McNeill Whistler; and Bellini's *Madonna and Child.*

In the end I opted for the Whistler painting because it appealed to me both visually and philosophically: it had the moodiness of a Lowry and made me want to see the world differently. One of the accompanying notes to the painting was a quote from Whistler, to the effect that during his time in the city he had 'learned to know a Venice that others never seem to have perceived'. Whistler's allusion to a more refined sensibility had me questioning my own perceptiveness of the world around me. Do I see the Britain that everyone else sees, or do I see my own version of that country? I decided that it was the former; that I too often wait to be directed to beauty and significance, rather than discovering them for myself. Next time I go looking, I decided, I'll go looking alone, and leave Bryson in the bathroom.

In any case, I saw something beautiful now – a mother and father having a whispered argument in front of Rodin's sculpture *The Thinker*, he in red, she in black, their child in-between staring up at Rodin's thoughtful subject. Given that I had seen a fair amount of Venice in recent years, and given that it was the day before Christmas Eve and I was longing to see my own parents, I returned the Whistler painting and took that family scene home instead. It would be my final souvenir, my journey's token, and it would be so because its content – a loving dispute in the midst of greatness – spoke quietly and imperfectly of Britain.

But I had one more call to make. One more stop before the journey was done. I had to find the man responsible for all this. I had to find Bill.

8 January 2014

Dear Ben,

I am very sorry I wasn't in Wramplingham when you called, but we don't live there any more. We moved about a month before you got there.

I have just looked at your introductory video and it's excellent – very professional and engaging, and much too kind to me. I am grateful to you for your generous words about my book. I'm afraid I can't read your blog because I am about to engage on a similar exercise of revisiting much of that territory myself and I can't risk allowing your observations to colour or influence mine. I must remain ignorant of where you went and stayed, what you encountered and concluded and all the rest. I do hope you had an excellent adventure, however, and that it was a mostly heartening experience. Britain is still, I think, the best and loveliest of countries. It is why I choose to live here. I hope you found it so, too.

Good luck with the rest of your life and best wishes for all you do.

Yours sincerely,

Bill Bryson

Acknowledgements

I would like to thank everyone at Icon (my editor Ellen Conlon especially) and everyone who supported *Dear Bill Bryson* when it was first dangled on the internet in 2015 like a dubious carrot. For some reason, when that first edition was published, I chose to acknowledge both the supporter and what they most recently had for dinner. I can't see why I shouldn't do the same here. John Wells; scrambled eggs. Daniel Monaghan; vegan mince. J.Y. Lam; curry. Kate Manning; gnocchi and chocolate. Meg Dobson; salmon, sweet potato mash and mangetout. Susan Roggendorf; salmon tartine. Matt Hudson; an entire roast chicken and English mustard. James Lamont; curry. Thomas James Aitken; spaghetti bolognaise. James Tweddle; sushi. Theresa Braun; fries and wine. Michael Bonsall; spinach. Jen Pacheco; squirrel. Julian D. Willis; Chinese. Sam Ryan; stir-fry. Nicola Graham; lamb rump with pea purée and rosemary and red wine jus. Mark Tate; Coopers Pale Ale. Morgan Hamilton-Griffin; burgers and pulled pork. Rachel Nisbet; mixed fruit crumble. Patricia Michelson; poached fish. Matt Alcock; a tasting menu. Andreas Kraft; half a cheese sandwich. Denise; half a cheese sandwich. Matt Wayne; chilli. Jörg Mattusch; pizza. Howard Hutt; cheese and tomato sandwich. Alicia Payne; chicken and rice. Steve Dews; kebab. Anthony Ford-Shubrook; beer and sausages. James Marsden; two-dozen mussels. Craig Marshall; pizza. Anna Topczewska; tacos. Arvid Klein Gregersen; lasagne. Gizem Guney; beef mince. Jo Patterson; a smiling Cheshire cat. Joris Beijers; fries with Belgian mayonnaise. Rebecca Wright; carrots and kale. Dave Walker; Cornish pasty. Paul Sobon; cold slice of leftover pizza. Tessa King; pannenkoeken. Ashley Allen; went hungry. Laura Schülke; sushi. Robert Stevens; cheeseburger with fries. Rachel Lothian; pasta. Marg Allen; wine. Peter and Sue Lucas; green Thai chicken curry. Octavia Horgan; CHICKEN! Jay Cunnington; lobster, biltong, mushy peas and a goblet of Pepsi. Michelle Wilson; roasted vegetables. Tom Judge; meat. Aimee King; kung pao chicken. Samuel Labib; bacon sandwich. Ruby Wand; kale and quinoa salad. Liz Slade; beer and quiche. Sue Gridley; chilli. Simon Havard; tzatziki. Idil Orhon; mushrooms. Roman Hermanek; nothing. Kevin and Lisa White; ice cream and crisps. William Daniels; milk. Aaron Sandler; Aaron Sandler. Lauren Pilkington; pizza. Katie Griffin; naughty Year 7s. Ben Rees; salad. Matt Ryan; microwave meal for one. Katie Lundstrom; salmon taco. Rebecca Souster; miso soup. Usha Patel; lemon curd on toast. Hannah Boldt; mozzarella and penne. Wendy and Colin Mills; cured meats and port. Chris Chappell; trout and new potatoes. Santiago Lemoine; cigarettes. Nicola Tate; donuts and tofu. Russell Hickman; sweets. Dominique Lucas; fettuccine puttanesca. Steve Chappell; coq au vin. Ian Baguley; broccoli and tomato ketchup. Mike Edwards; mince and mealie pie. Steve Benzie; whisky. Chris Phillips; chicken nuggets. Shelly Williams; Fate's leftovers. Michael Lamont; phaal. Thomas Frederick Aitken; meat and two veg then trifle. Jayne Lamont and Ian Ricketts; casserole. Sylvia and Alan; KFC. Yvonne and Bob Robertson; burritos. Brendon Bostock; frozen veg, chicken breast, rice, chilli sauce. Gabriella Swerling; flat white and biscuits.

ABOUT THE AUTHOR

Ben Aitken was born under Thatcher, grew to six foot then stopped, and is an Aquarius. He is the author of *A Chip Shop in Poznań: My Unlikely Year in Poland* (2019), *The Gran Tour: Travels with my Elders* (2020) and *The Marmalade Diaries: A True Story of an Odd Couple* (2022).

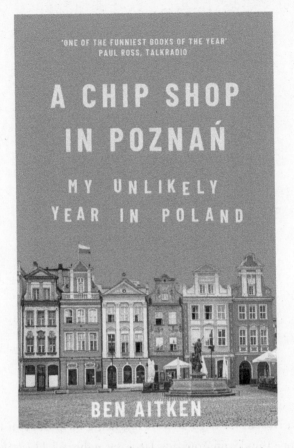

'One of the funniest books of the year'
– Paul Ross, talkRADIO

WARNING: CONTAINS AN UNLIKELY IMMIGRANT,
AN UNSUNG COUNTRY, A BUMPY ROMANCE, SEVERAL
SHATTERED PRECONCEPTIONS, TRACES OF INSIGHT,
A DOZEN NUNS AND A REFERENDUM.

9781785786266
£9.99

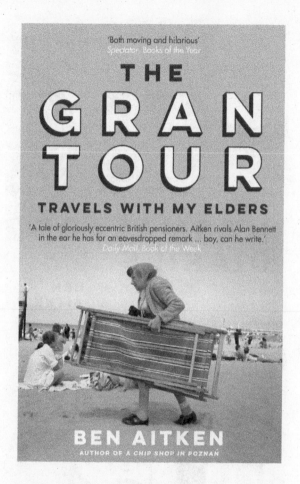

'Both moving and hilarious'
Spectator, Books of the Year

THE
GRAN
TOUR

TRAVELS WITH MY ELDERS

'A tale of gloriously eccentric British pensioners. Aitken rivals Alan Bennett
in the ear he has for an eavesdropped remark ... boy, can he write.'
Daily Mail, Book of the Week

BEN AITKEN
AUTHOR OF A CHIP SHOP IN POZNAŃ

'A tale of gloriously eccentric British pensioners
and a light-hearted travelogue ... but so much more
than that as well. The pen portraits of his fellow
holidaymakers are wonderful. And boy, can he write.'

– Daily Mail

9781785787041
£9.99

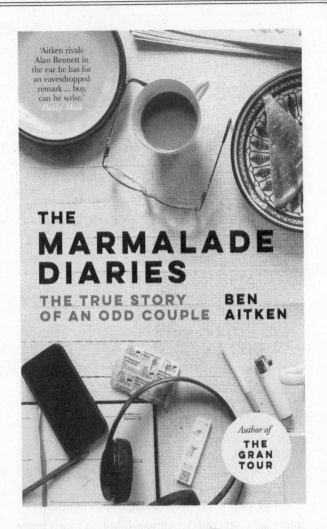

'Aitken rivals Alan Bennett in the ear he has for an eavesdropped remark ... boy, can he write.'
Daily Mail

THE
MARMALADE DIARIES
THE TRUE STORY OF AN ODD COUPLE

BEN AITKEN

Author of
THE GRAN TOUR

One house. Two housemates. Three reasons
to worry: Winnie and Ben are separated by 50 years,
a gulf in class, and major differences of opinion.

9781785788130
Hardback: £16.99